IMAGES
of Canada

OLDE TYME CHRISTMAS IN
NEW BRUNSWICK

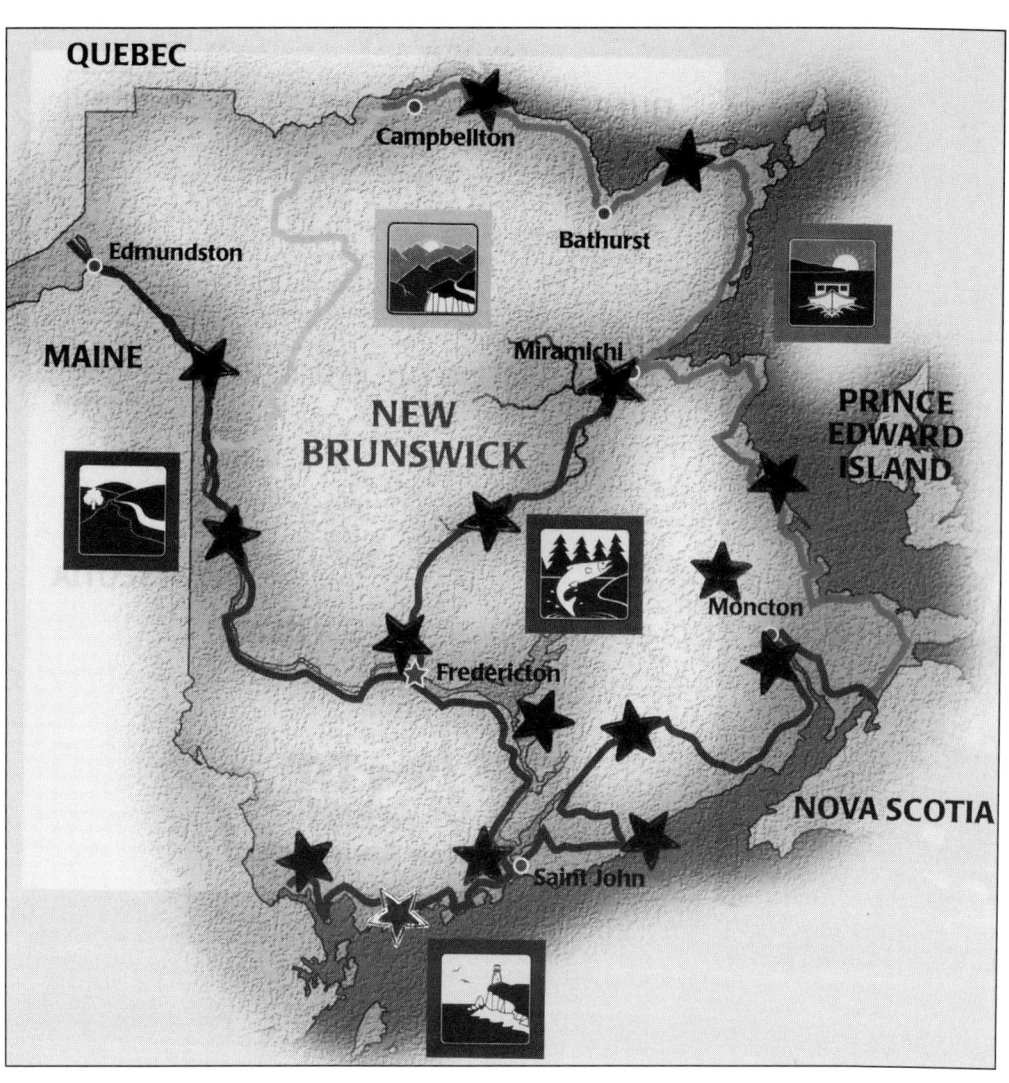

QUEBEC

Campbellton

Edmundston

Bathurst

MAINE

Miramichi

NEW
BRUNSWICK

PRINCE
EDWARD
ISLAND

Moncton

Fredericton

NOVA SCOTIA

Saint John

IMAGES
of Canada

OLDE TYME CHRISTMAS IN
NEW BRUNSWICK

David Goss

ARCADIA

First published 1997
Copyright © David Goss, 1997

ISBN 0-7524-0523-3

Published by Arcadia Publishing,
an imprint of the Chalford Publishing Corporation,
One Washington Center, Dover, New Hampshire 03820.
Printed in Great Britain

Library of Congress Cataloging-in-Publication Data applied for

Contents

Acknowledgments

All of the photos have been credited with the exception of those from my own collection. Should a picture be miscredited or inadvertently used from a private collection that I was unable to identify, I apologize, and it will be corrected in a later printing. I deeply appreciate the loan of photos and trust that those selected from the many I borrowed will be pleasing to the people who furnished them to me. In order to provide maximum descriptive material for the pictures, some credits are shortened and the following legend will indicate ownership.

Public Agencies:
*PA P#-# New Brunswick Provincial Archives P.O. Box 6000, Fredericton, E3B 5H1. This is a public agency open to all. Many New Brunswickers do not know of the rich collection of heritage photos that are available to them at this source. Anyone with historic photos should consider making them available for future generations through this agency.

Private collectors that have provided several photos:
*HW: refers to Harold E. Wright of 1 Chipman Hill, Saint John, NB, E2L 2A7, who has provided photos from his collections as identified.
*Vintage Photo and Frame refers to Wilson Studio Collection, c/o Grant Kelly, 110 Prince William Street, Saint John, NB, E2L 2P3.
*Nurses Association of New Brunswick refers to Nursing History Resource Centre, courtesy of Arlee Hoyt McGee, Nurse Archivist, 165 Regent Street, Fredericton, E3B 7B4.
*N.B.P.O.H refers to New Brunswick Protestant Orphans Home at 66 Waterloo Street, Saint John, NB, E2L 3P4.
*Canadian Red Cross refers to the New Brunswick Division of the Canadian Red Cross, 405 University Avenue, P.O. Box 39, Saint John, NB, E2L 3X3.

If there is an image owned by the any of the above that is of interest, they may be able to provide a copy, so contact them directly. Other images identified throughout the book may also be available. Addresses are available from the author, David Goss, 21 Glenwood Drive, Saint John, NB, E2M 5P3, or call (506) 672-8601.

For assistance with the copying of photos, I am indebted to Grant Kelly, of Vintage Photo and Frame; Rob Roy, of Rob Roy Productions; and Sandra Kenny, of Black's Photo. For manuscript preparation and assistance, I acknowledge the help of my son, Derek Goss.

Introduction

What is an "olde tyme" Christmas? Essentially, it is anything we have done to celebrate the season that we're sentimentally attached to. Thus, it could be the neighbourhood party we sponsored last year that becomes a tradition and forges a link with the past. Almost everything we do to celebrate Christmas was begun this way. This has been happening ever since the Romans celebrated the return of the sun at the Saturnalia Festivals before the Christian era. We can link our use of greens to this time, and we know the early Church modeled their celebrations after this Roman festivity when they marked the birth of Jesus.

To them it seemed more sensible to borrow and build upon an established tradition than to invent a new one. Thus, the focus gradually shifted from the solar sun to the Son of God. In 350 AD, Pope Julius I declared December 25th as Christmas.

Over the centuries the festival gradually picked up all the elements of Christmas as we know it now: the feasting, caroling, veneration of St. Nicholas, the exchange of presents, the decorating of church and home, the candles in the windows, the creche in the town squares, the reaching out to the poor, the enjoyment of heart-tugging stories, the staging of plays and pageants, the enjoyment of Christmas musicals, the community parades, etc. These have all developed in different places and at different times since Christ's birth as standardized ways to enjoy the festive season almost everywhere in the world.

However, some of the festive elements of the past, including gambling, rowdy sports, card playing, begging, mumming, carousing, and offering monetary tribute to the king and clergy, became so debased that between 1647 and 1660 Christmas was banned. Those who dared to celebrate would be placed in jail.

Christmas could not be kept down, though, and soon the old ideas were picked up, reshaped, and began to grow, especially in England. During the reign of Queen Victoria (1837–1901), many ideas like caroling, feasting, and mumming were revived, and many new elements, the decorated tree, Christmas cards, the ghost story, pantomime and Christmas pageants, the cracker, and the visit of St. Nicholas, emerged. Especially important at this time was the growing idea that Christmas was to be a festival for children, not adults. Britain domination of the world in the nineteenth century meant that these ideas travelled widely, and people who emigrated from England and wanted a bit of home at Christmas adapted the ideas in the far-off colonies, including Canada. Today, when people think of an old-fashioned Christmas, it is generally the ideas developed in the Victorian era. Thus, enjoying snowy scenes, sleigh rides, and evergreen-bedecked churches, helping of the poor, hanging stockings and exchanging gifts, going to Midnight Mass, savouring the Gospel stories of Jesus' birth, listening to Dickens's tales, having a visit from Santa, caroling on the green, and eating lots of turkey, mince pies, and plum puddings are Christmas images held in common throughout the world.

In this collection of over 200 images, we explore how the British ideas of Christmas moved into New Brunswick. This look is made possible through the clippings and photographs New Brunswickers have generously lent and augmented by commentary gleaned from diaries, scrapbooks, newspapers, and periodicals of yesteryear that were known and enjoyed in New Brunswick at the time the photos were taken. This, then, is Christmas and how it has been marked in New Brunswick from the Victorian age to the television age. In the images there will be familiar faces and places, and some will take the reader back in time to his or her youth, or that of their parents or grandparents. It is hoped these images of the season will remind each reader of some element of the Christmas season that may have been forgotten. Some of the photos may encourage the reader to reintroduce a long forgotten custom of their youth, or start a new tradition that will make Christmas today more meaningful. If that is accomplished only once or twice in the 128 pages that follow, then the months of work arranging this volume into the story of Christmas past in New Brunswick will have been worthwhile.

David Goss,
February 27, 1997

One

An Overview of the Festive Season

Winter at the Barracks in Fredericton. Fredericton, with its regularly changing regiments from the British Isles, was at the forefront of celebrating the growth of Christmas in North America. It was in Fredericton that many of New Brunswick's firsts in connection with Christmas occurred: the Christmas tree was first seen in these barracks, and on the streets nearby, Santa made his first appearance delivering gifts. Thus, Fredericton gets placed first as we begin our discovery of the festive season in New Brunswick. How the holiday developed and how it was celebrated will be seen via the 200-plus pictures to follow made available from those who love the season in every part of the province. (Courtesy of PA P 37-345.)

Hanging the Greens. The first Christmases in New Brunswick would not make as an attractive picture as this one from a nineteenth-century greeting card. Any family that could dress like these folks would likely have had servants to drape the greens. For most early settlers, Christmas was just another day and often a workday, because farm chores were never ending.

THE SEASON'S GREETINGS

The Yule Log Tradition. Gathering wood for various purposes was a way of life in New Brunswick as will be seen in the sections to follow. Gathering Yule Logs was a tradition of the Old Country that did not cross the ocean to North America except as an idea on the greeting cards and calling cards that circulated in the latter part of the nineteenth century. Many other traditions did resurface in New Brunswick and will be seen in the wood carvings, illustrations, and engravings to follow.

Fire at York Point, Christmas, 1854. Though Edward Anthony photographed the St. Croix River in 1840 to settle a border dispute and John Fletcher lectured in the Saint John Mechanics Institute on photography that same year, we depend on drawings and paintings for most illustrations of Christmas in the province before 1890. (Courtesy of *Daily Telegraph*, 1893.)

Left: First New Brunswick Nativity Drawing. The sacred side of Christmas wasn't as developed as is generally assumed in the Victorian era. Few cards contained religious themes, and many churches did not hold services at Christmas. The church's role at Christmas will become clear in the chapters on churches, on the trees of Christmas, on Santa, and how the three interacted. (Courtesy of *Fredericton Capital*, December 24, 1887.)

Right: An Early Engraving of Santa. Santa's image also appeared in the Fredericton papers on the same page as the Nativity on December 24, 1887. Santa's changing appearance from then until now will be clarified in a chapter on the old gent beginning on page 81.

The Church Choir. Though there was early resistance in some churches to the celebration of Christmas, many held special services, with well-rehearsed Christmas music. This cut comes from *Progress*, a Saint John paper that was known for using the latest in engraved images to show what was going on in the port city. To some degree, the same Christmas events happened in other cities, towns, and rural areas as this collection of photos will show.

Duncan Family at Christmas 1911. Though schools and churches started to decorate with trees in the 1870s, many families thought it a bit silly to have a tree in their homes when there were so many standing just outside. By the 1900s, conditions had changed and the custom was growing quickly. Also, the idea of the family portrait with the tree as a background became a popular mainstay, as many of our pictures to follow show. (Courtesy of Vintage Photo and Frame #9989.)

A Survey Crew Takes a Rest. Through the book, you will see where men and women shopped, worked, and played. Many of the snapshots of workers will show rugged, burly men, such as this crew on the Stanley Road at Boiestown, New Brunswick. They were about to break for Christmas on December 19, 1904. The crew engineer is C.L. Foss, who travelled to all corners of the province laying out roads, bridges, dams, and rail lines. (Courtesy of Geoff Foss.)

A Precious Cargo. One of the reasons winter was welcome in times past was the ease of travel that sleighs permitted. Though seldom seen today, a sleigh ride remains one of the romantic images of Christmas. Members of the Pickett family enjoy a ride near their Woodman's Point home on the Long Reach of the St. John River around 1910. (Courtesy of Lorraine Pickett.)

A Stereoscopic View of Christmas at the Asylum. The charitable and benevolent societies, as well as those operating orphanages, missions, and asylums, tried to make Christmas special for their patients. Their efforts are seen in the chapters on churches and institutions, which also show more stereoscopic views of Centracare in Saint John decorated during Christmas 1911. (Courtesy of Nurses Association of New Brunswick.)

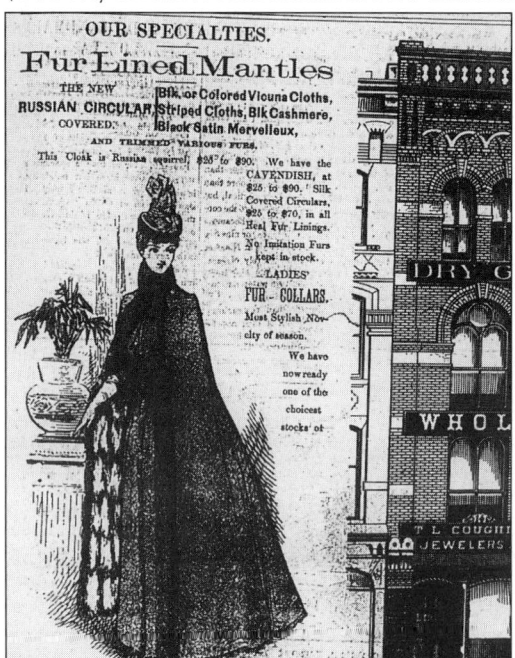

Left: Commercial Side of Christmas. About 1860, merchants discovered the financial benefits of promoting the growing custom of exchanging gifts. At this time, children became the focus of the Christmas celebration and the natural recipients of toys, games, and puzzles that began to be imported in larger quantities from England and America to complement homemade items.
Right: The Canadian Winter Girls. Marion McCluskey (left) and Marion Rice (right), two girls from the Miramichi, are representative of many of the robust generation of yesteryear who used sleds, skates, skis, and snowshoes to enjoy the outdoors at Christmas and through the rest of the long winter. (Courtesy of Central New Brunswick Woodmen's Museum.)

Two
A Glimpse at How
New Brunswick Looked

Sleighing on Harris Street, Saint John. *Sketches of New Brunswick*, published in London in 1856, commented: "The winter in New Brunswick is a season of great activity. The snow renders many parts of the country accessible which from want of good roads are almost impassable in summer." In this chapter and in the next, we shall see what the provinces, cities, and rural areas looked like primarily in the era before efficient snow clearing that is the norm today. This sleigh running down Harris Street in 1916 in the North End of Saint John would not have appreciated the mechanical plow essential to the Christmas traveller of today. (Courtesy of HW: O'Leary collection PA P 375.)

A Procession of Sleighs in Loggieville. As Christmas approached in the nineteenth century, there were preparations that required visits to the nearest town or city. Shops would remain open until late Christmas Eve. While most came in from rural areas by sleigh, such as this group arriving in Loggieville, some used the train service joining many communities, and once in town there were streetcars in Moncton, Saint John, and St. Stephen. (Courtesy of PA P 25-46.)

Streetcar Travel in St. Stephen. The Town of St. Stephen shared a 7-mile street railway with the City of Calais, Maine, from 1894 to 1929. What a thrill it must have been to youngsters who were used to horse-drawn wagons and sleighs to ride on iron rails as they did their Christmas shopping in the big town. Saint John streetcars are seen on pages 31 and 34. (Courtesy PA P 128-79.)

16

Newcastle Town Square. This photograph, taken by Ole Larsen, is of the reconstructed Newcastle Town Square, now known as Miramichi City, after a disastrous fire in the late 1890s had destroyed the previous buildings. Fires in times past were common, and no city escaped their terror. This photo would have been carefully posed for because any movement in the picture would have resulted in blurring due to the time exposure necessary to capture the image; thus, many pre-twentieth-century photos do not have persons posing in them. (Courtesy of PA P 6-115.)

Snowy Moncton. Moncton residents have traditionally had to deal with much more snow than most other sections of New Brunswick. Though this photograph is from a March 1923 storm, it is representative of the conditions in Moncton at Christmas time in most years. (Courtesy of PA P 75-26C.)

East End Tenements, Saint John. A century ago, central Saint John had a solid, yet decorative look, for all the buildings were brick as a result of a city bylaw imposed following the great fire of 1877. Many residents, however, lived in nearby wooden tenements in the Brussel, St. Patrick, and St. David Street areas. In 1883 the huge cotton mill, visible in the background, opened and some four hundred of the mostly Irish immigrants who had settled in the area found work. (Courtesy of Geoff Foss.)

Lumber at Long Wharf, Saint John. Lumber was the driving force in the economy through the nineteenth century, as this scene at Saint John's Long Wharf area attests. Loading the deals for shipment overseas provided steady paychecks. The typical labourer in the late nineteenth century earned between $7 and $10 for a 60-hour workweek. (Courtesy of the mayor's office, Saint John.)

Saint John Snowbanks. Outside of the brick structures area of Saint John were the wooden tenements of the lower South End and East End. This girl is waiting for her mother on Pitt Street, from where they would walk ten minutes to the uptown stores to do some Christmas shopping. (Courtesy of Victor Duffy.)

Left: When the Pitt Street girl reached the city centre, walking conditions would not have been much better, as shown by these snowbanks near the Masonic Temple. These snowbanks were being removed by horse-drawn plows in this turn-of-the-century photograph.
Right: The MacIntyres found this old photograph in the Rowen House in the North End when they took over the building in the 1950s. (Both pictures courtesy of Jack and Elsie MacIntyre.)

A New Winter Coat to Show Off! Fredericton usually received a lot more snow than Saint John. However, when Patricia (Cameron) Kindred posed in this park opposite Waterloo Row in her Christmas finery in the early 1950s, there was little snow. In the 1880s in this park, a Quebec firm built a tall snow slide that permitted toboggans to slide well out onto the frozen St. John River to the east of the Legislative buildings. (Courtesy of Mary Ellen Kindred.)

Downtown Fredericton: a City of Small Shops. A number of these images from A.V.F. Duffy show the three cities of New Brunswick as Duffy traveled around the province on his honeymoon in 1922. These shots give us a view of the structures that the citizens of the time knew. Small family businesses in Fredericton, such as Hall's bookstore, Oak Hall, Lamont's Variety store, and J.J. Waddall, are long gone. A few downtown Fredericton shops of the early 1900s will be seen on pages 94–96. (Courtesy of Victor Duffy.)

Moncton: New Brunswick's Railtown. The "subway" in Moncton still exists, but today it carries diesel locomotives, not steam trains as in this 1921 shot. Anyone who wanted to shop in downtown Moncton had to pass under the "subway" in order to get to the central city shops. (Courtesy of Victor Duffy.)

The T. Eaton Catalogue Centre. Thousands of New Brunswickers never saw the T.E. Eaton company, but they knew of the firm from the goods they could order and have delivered to their homes. From this plant, goods were shipped to all points in the Maritime provinces. The fact that Mr. Duffy took time from his honeymoon to take the photo indicates he must have been a satisfied customer. (Courtesy of Victor Duffy.)

A Company Store in a Company Town. Shoppers in Blacks Harbour had the Conner Bros. Ltd. in which to do their shopping. This company built the town's water supply, an arena, and also many homes for their fish packing employees. Since 1954, they have annually arranged for Santa to visit the seaside village and present gifts to the children of the area on December 24th. The sleigh used on the visits is shown on page 88. (Courtesy of Victor Duffy.)

Over the Border Shopping in Maine. Slipping over the border to shop for American Christmas goods in the city of Calais wasn't considered as unpatriotic or an anti-government a statement as it seems to be today. A.V.F. Duffy took this photograph of Calais in 1921. Hard hit by fires over the years, Calais is a mere shadow of what he captured in this picture. (Courtesy of Victor Duffy.)

Ladies in a Lumber Camp! Shocking! There was a huge section of the population of New Brunswick who were hard at work in the woods from late November until the rivers opened up in the spring. In this photo are the crews in the St. Leonard area with female visitors. It was unusual to see a lady in a lumber camp. Some old-timers have speculated that they may have been invited to a Christmas dance, but more likely, they felt, it was the wife and family of the owner, who were brought out to visit on a Sunday afternoon. (Courtesy of PA P 51-38.)

Procession in Albert County. Though this photo is identified as being Lower Corner, Albert County, this is more likely to have been Lower Cape, Albert County, according to those who know the area. This scene, taken from the Harvey side, is of a winter procession; the occasion is unknown. The train has been loaded with logs from the mill located out of the picture to the left of the homes. (Courtesy of PA P 69-18.)

Ice Cream in Winter? The Kent County Historical Society collection provided this photo of a winter gathering in Buctouche. There seems to be a banner hanging from the local hotel and spanning the street which was lettered after the photo was taken with "E.C. Collett." Collett apparently used this photograph in promoting ice cream, probably as part of a winter carnival. (Courtesy of PA P 78-86.)

Longest Covered Bridge in the World in Winter. The Hartland Covered Bridge is pictured often in New Brunswick summer promotional literature, but few have visited it in winter. In order to sleigh over covered bridges in the winter, residents would have to line the inside roadway with snow. This would be a difficult task in Hartland, as the bridge is 1,282 feet long. (Courtesy of Doris Kennedy.)

Senator King's Kingdom, Chipman, 1908. The village of Chipman in 1908 was a lumber town that depended on the Salmon River (in the foreground) for shipment of raw materials downriver. It was via this river that Chipman was connected to the world by riverboat in the earliest times. Senator George Gerald King built up quite a business in the area. Behind the house is the smokestack for the power and heating plant he owned. His mansion stood behind his general store until the 1960s. (Thanks to Carol Kuehner for this postcard's background.)

Charlotte Street in Saint John. This photograph of Charlotte Street was taken from the corner of Duke Street on December 27, 1933. Note that traffic is still moving both ways on what is now a one-way street and that there is but a single street lamp on this long stretch of Charlotte Street. The 1925 Admiral Beatty Hotel shows on the top right, and across King's Square is a King Cole Tea sign, which could be seen until the Bank of Nova Scotia was constructed in 1939. (Courtesy of HW: Malcolm collection PIRP 7618.)

Commercial Hub of Province-Market Slip, Saint John. Turn-of-the-century Christmas postcards didn't necessarily depict Christmas themes, but also presented well-known attractions, such as this one of the Loyalist landing site at Market Slip in Saint John. Almost every commercial product sold in New Brunswick was landed at or near Market Slip in the days of wooden ships and steamboat travel in the province. The photo is undoubtedly an Erb Print from around 1908. (Courtesy of Marilyn Galbraith.)

Saint John's Winter Pleasure Place. Rockwood Park shown in this postcard was a popular Christmas playground for Saint John residents. It was a great spot for nighttime sleigh riders and anyone who liked looking down over winking gas lamps of the city centre. The lake would be black with skaters on Christmas afternoon when conditions permitted. This is also an Erb photograph taken between 1908 and 1913. (Courtesy of Marilyn Galbraith.)

Three
How Folks Got from Place to Place

Mrs. Robert Mitchell's Sleigh Ride, Saint John. In Saint John at Christmas, those who had not pre-booked and prepaid for a sleigh for Christmas afternoon would not be able to get one. In this instance, Mrs. Robert Mitchell has hired a sleigh from Watson Stables located on 91–95 Duke Street for her family and friends. She lived in the shadow of the Cathedral where this picture was likely taken. The family was probably off to one of the popular locations for sleighing: out Manawagonish Road in west Saint John to a spot overlooking Taylor's Island or out the old Marsh Road to Three Mile House where refreshments could be procured. Rockwood Park was always a popular destination and as creepy as it might seem, so was Fernhill Cemetery. (Courtesy of Vintage Photo and Frame.)

Moose on the Loose!! New Brunswick folktales tell of moose being tamed to work in yarding operations in the woods and moose being so clever that when their master was downed by a fallen tree, they would push the deadfall off the injured person. These could be dismissed as Saturday night stories, legends, or tall tales; however, this picture clearly shows a moose harnessed for duty. It was found in the Woodbridge Collection, indicating it was likely taken in the Fredericton area. In addition, there is a story and photo in the *North Shore Leader* of April 22, 1949, of a moose tamed by John Connell in Big Bartiboque, Northumberland County. Mr. Connell and his partner Daniel Lloyd caught the moose in deep snow at the end of winter and trained it to haul his sleigh into Chatham, some 11 miles south, where it was quite an attraction. This article also notes that in 1871 the governor of New Brunswick had a trained moose according to a report published in Dublin that year. (Courtesy of PA P 32-23.)

Baby's First Outing, St. George. Sleighs came in a great variety of styles and were in use all over the province for basic transportation and for tasks like hauling cut ice, bales of hay, lumber, etc. Here we have Margaret, Roy, and Roberta (the baby) Spinney enjoying a pleasure trip outside St. George on February 23, 1945. (Courtesy of Elizabeth Toy.)

Quick Change Artist's Sleigh. The unidentified driver of this sleigh in the Hartland, New Brunswick area in 1913 or 1914–15 seems to have devised some way of quickly converting his conveyance from a sleigh to a buggy. This is a practical idea in New Brunswick, especially in the south, where changeable winters are the norm. It is an idea still used today in Saint John, where sleigh rides often become wagon rides during snow-free times. (Courtesy of Doris Kennedy.)

A Sunday Outing for the Sipprelle Family. The Sunday sleigh of Scott and Elizabeth Sipprelle of Hartland was taken out only on special occasions, such as Christmas and to church. It is a two-seater, polished brightly and sporting bells. The fur coats, collars, and muffs on display were all handmade in Hartland at Keith and Plummer Ltd., which was the popular shopping destination in Hartland at the turn of the century. (Courtesy of Doris Kennedy.)

Moose! Horses! Now Oxen Pulling the Sleigh! A team of oxen has arrived outside the Keith and Plummer store. The store's highlight at Christmas time was the tunes from a music box that continually played carols for the shoppers. Another attraction was the pot-bellied stove where old-timers gathered to share stories. On Christmas Eve, shoppers stayed as late as necessary, and if they had no way home, the store owner would provide a ride. (Courtesy of Doris Kennedy.)

Sleighs Had a Practical Side, Too. Sleigh rides developed from the practical side of owning horses and their ability to ease the workload of the owner. One of the daily tasks in Bristol was hauling barrels of potatoes to the Christmas market. David Foulton (left) and Thomas Darleis (right) are the workers in charge of this load. (Courtesy of Doris Kennedy.)

Relotte's Horse . . . But Who Was Relotte? C.L. Foss was an engineer who planned rail beds, roads, and dams in New Brunswick, and among his pictures is this one that he has meticulously numbered. Unfortunately, as sometimes happens, the key to the numbering was lost in the Foss papers. All that remains on the back of the photo is that this was Relotte's horse in front of Res #13. (Courtesy of Geoff Foss.)

A Gang of Sleighs for Orphan Kids. The New Brunswick Protestants Orphanage Home in Fairville, a suburb of Saint John West, was conscious of the fact that children in their care should enjoy a loving Christmas experience, and they annually arranged sleighs to provide a ride around the Manawagonish Road and Quinton Heights property in Saint John. (See also page 119–121 for more orphanage photos.) (Courtesy of NBPOH.)

Two Tracks Begin to Beat Four Hooves. As motor vehicles replaced horses, there were many innovative vehicles put together by clever mechanics trying to create transportation as reliable as the horse had been. This is Armstrong Garage's attempt from the D. Johnson collection. (Courtesy of PA P 29-28.)

The Iron Horse at Bayshore Station. Much more reliable than the snow trackers and the variations of the chassis of the Model T's and Model A's was train service. This engine is awaiting duties at the Bayshore yard on the west side of Saint John. In 1883 a Christmas Eve train out of Moncton was reported to have had a tree decorated with oranges, apples, and empty liquor bottles set up in honour of a bride and groom on the train. (Courtesy of Victor Duffy.)

Streetcar Decked out for the Holidays. Though this streetcar looks dressed for Christmas, it was actually decorated for a 1923 winter carnival. It must have been quite a sight to see it lit up by four hundred bulbs as it drove up King Street, where the city held its winter carnival and where there was a huge ice arch. Also, Miss Winnifred Blair of the port city, the first Miss Canada ever crowned, was here on her throne. (Courtesy of HW: Belyea collection PIRP 4626.)

Shopper's Express . . . the Saint John Streetcar! Streetcar #33 makes its way along Duke Street in Saint John. The spire of St. Andrews Church is seen in the background. Streetcars were seldom stopped by storms. The New Brunswick Power Company had its own track cleaning equipment to ensure everyone got to work and the ladies could reach their shopping destinations in the morning hours and get back home in time to prepare the children's noon-time meal. (Courtesy of HW: Malcolm collection PIRP 7631.)

Four

The Christmas Tree

An 1807 account of Christmas in New Brunswick written to friends in England by Lady Hunter mentions sleighing and hanging stockings and gifts left by Queen Mab, a fairy. Historian Clarence Ward wrote in 1898 of how he imagined Christmas in 1808; he mentions lots of fine foods, great quantities of liquor, turkey shoots on Christmas morning, long church services, and afternoons devoted to games. Early accounts in the *New Brunswick Courier* mention long breaks for schoolchildren, starting in 1818, and that children took exams for which prizes were awarded. In 1830 Clement Moore's "Twas the Night Before Christmas" was printed in the *New Brunswick Courier*. What is missing from all these accounts? There is no mention of the use of a tree, a standard part of the Christmas celebration today. So how did trees reach New Brunswick? We will discover in this chapter how the first trees were introduced by the members of the regiments in Fredericton in the early 1860s and how they gradually became so popular that by the turn of the century, about 25% of the population could pose for pictures, as this couple from Quaco did in 1905. The Quaco Historical Society identified the lady as Gladys Brown. (Courtesy of PA P 22-178.)

Luther's Candlelit Tree. We go back to the German story of how Martin Luther was walking through the winter woods and so enjoyed the twinkling of starlight through the trees that he took one inside his house and bedecked it with candles to entrance his children. This idea eventually spread to New Brunswick.

Queen Victoria Embraces Christmas. Our next link to the introduction of the tree is through Queen Victoria with her family in a cut from the *Illustrated London News* in 1848. This drawing spread around the world and encouraged families to raise trees to imitate the Royal Family. The first time this is reported in New Brunswick is in the early 1860s when the 22nd Regiment gathered for supper at the Fredericton headquarters (see also page 9). The room was said to have been tastefully decorated with evergreens, with the chief attraction being an enormous tree in the centre of the room.

Bachelor's Christmas Reverie. The idea of Christmas trees remained one for schools, churches, and businesses to use for nearly forty years. Imagery of old time Christmas from the *Daily Telegraph* shows stockings hung by the fire with a game of Blind Man's Buff being played and the greens tucked behind pictures everywhere in this room as the old fellow dreams, but there is still no tree. The chapter on "Shops" beginning on page 89 will show how decorations were used in stores. (Courtesy of *Saint John Daily Telegraph*, December 24, 1892.)

Baby's First Christmas. The oldest image of a tree found in researching this book is from the year 1900. It is identified as "Baby's First Christmas" on the back. Scott and Elizabeth Sipprelle at Victoria Corner, 3 miles from Hartland, had trees like this. Mr. Sipprelle was a blacksmith, a barber, and a farmer. He would have also made the horse rocker and horse-drawn wagon. His wife would have made the strings of popcorn and cranberries and rolled the cornucopias, perhaps of old wallpaper, and the tin drum and celluloid doll tied to the top of the tree would have come from Keith and Plummer in Hartland. (Courtesy of Doris Kennedy.)

A Tabletop Tree, 1900. The same year as Baby's First Christmas, at the other end of the province, Leonard and Dorothy Smith of Grangeville, Kent County, were photographed by their father H.W.B. Smith while admiring their tabletop tree. Grangeville was little more than a clearing in the woods at the time, so it seems strange that the ornaments on this tree aren't handmade, but are all printed cards that would have been relatively expensive at the time. H.W.B. Smith was a roving photographer who travelled by train all over the counties of southern New Brunswick and likely picked up the decorative material in Moncton. (Courtesy of Mrs. Claude Babcock.)

Trinkets under the Tree. The Smith tree also appears to have store-bought gifts. Mrs. Claude Babcock of Elgin, the photographer's granddaughter, has a problem with this because the family does not believe there was much money available at the time. The rich collection of photographs left behind by Mr. Smith (which show up throughout this book), the fact that her grandfather owned a camera, and his ability to travel extensively suggest that there was some financial security beyond farming. (Courtesy of Mrs. Claude Babcock.)

Where, Oh Where, to Place the Tree? This vexing question comes up in every home as it did in the Rowen family, who built a fine four-square home on the peninsula along the lower part of the Saint John River overlooking Marble Cove in the year 1898. This was a fancy home as can be seen from the grillwork in the living room. The tree was placed in the corner to the extreme right. (Courtesy of Jack and Elsie MacIntyre.)

40

The Rowen Tree, 1904. When Jack and Elsie MacIntyre moved into the Rowen home in 1962, they paid $50 for all the remnants that had been left behind by Jenny and Jackson Rowen. Among his finds when he explored the house was a scrapbook containing a photographic history of the house, the city, and even places in Europe that this well-off family had visited. One of the photos is this Christmas tree in 1904. The ornamentation of this tree is clearly store-bought material: chromolithographic cards, Tom Smith's famous crackers, gilded cornucopias, decorative globes, and clip-on and pendant-balanced candles. The gifts under the tree suggest a young girl had just been visited by Santa. (Courtesy of Jack and Elsie MacIntyre.)

CHRISTMAS 1911

Christmas Came by Riverboat. This is an excellent example of a tree decorated almost exclusively with home-produced material—the doll, perhaps being brought up from Saint John on a riverboat trip, being the obvious exception. The tree was photographed in the parlour of the Belyea home in Lower Cambridge on the Washademoak in 1911 and was likely taken by Harry Bulyea. Typical of the time was the use of family portraits as decorations on the walls and in the tree. The lily (to the left of tree) and the chrysanthemum were the most popular flower before the poinsettia became the choice for Christmas after World War II. (Courtesy of Gary Hughes.)

Under the Belyea Tree. The toys under the Belyea tree in 1911 are definitely store bought. Prices for a dressed doll could run from $1 to $7, depending on the quality, movability of the doll, and the number of changes of clothes included. The sheep and the dog were inexpensive, probably 10¢ to 25¢ each. They represented the rural life of the area, but the animals could also be part of a Noah's Ark, which was the most popular Christmas toy and the only toy allowed to be played with on Sunday. The dish set fits in with the idea that a young lady should learn domestic duties as part of her play. (Courtesy of Gary Hughes.)

A Doll for a Doll! Here we see Lorraine Pickett playing with a doll. Dolls were the most popular Christmas toy next to the Noah's Ark. On December 24, 1878, the *Saint John Globe* said, "Peek in almost any window on the streets where retail business is done and dolls may be seen of every kind and sort. There are dolls with lovely faces, hair that can be combed, and jointed fingers that will close. Eyes that can move energetically, dolls that can speak, and most charmingly dolls that can cry. There are dolls of bisque, rubber, china and wood in new and old form. As for boy dolls they are many and variously dressed and seem to be excellently behaved for boy dolls." (Courtesy of Lorraine Pickett.)

A.V.F. Duffy's Christmas Tree in 1916. On this tree there is a preference for the tinsel rope that had become popular at the turn of the century and strings of beads from Germany that made the stringing of cranberries a thing of the past in many homes. Note the tiny Santa in the centre of the tree. These were often given to children when the tree came down, so few have survived the passage of time. (Courtesy of Victor Duffy.)

Tinsel Flashback in an Era When Few Had Flash Cameras. By 1927, when this photo of the Pickett family was taken, tinsel had become a popular decorative material and presented obvious flash problems for the photographer. There seem to be few pictures of family events, church pageants, or Santa from this era, which is understandable because the Depression was on the horizon. (Courtesy of Lorraine Pickett.)

Two Contrasting Trees of Fifty Years Ago. Both of these photos are about a half century old, and as was the case early in this century, there is a wide discrepancy as to what is acceptable for a tree. The little fellow rocking (on the left) could be out of the *Better Homes and Gardens* magazine spread, but instead is in a Saint John home. Ann MacLeod (on the right), seen in the 1950s, is easily as picturesque in her Hartland home, though her tree and surroundings seem more in tune with how most folks celebrated Christmas in the war years. (Courtesy of Geoff Foss and Doris Kennedy.)

King's Square Tree Vendor. By the turn of the century, one in five homes would have a Christmas tree. On December 22, 1887, the *Daily Telegraph* reported: "Dealers in Christmas trees and evergreens began to gather around King's Square," which indicates there was a market for farm-cut trees by that time. There has been a good market for trees from the countryside ever since, and they are still sold annually in King's Square.

Trees for Export. A Growing Business in More Ways Than One! Landowners through the province discovered at the end of the last century that trees were needed in the American market. It was a Kings County man, George LeBar, who was known as "The Christmas Tree Man" and began shipping trees to his native Pennsylvania from Canada in 1898. In his best year, 1919, he shipped 265 railway flatcars. As is the case today, there were similar operations all over the province. The six gentlemen pictured here have some tall trees bailed and ready to go from their tree lot in the St. Leonard area. (Courtesy of LaPointe collection PA P 51-13.)

Bedroom Trees. By the 1930s, almost every home had a tree. It was customary for the tree to be put up in the parlour, and in many homes it was put up on the 24th and taken down on the 26th. Children who wished to have a tree for a longer time could sometimes have a small one in their room; such is the case with Art Pottle who lived on Thorne Avenue in east Saint John. (Courtesy of Art Pottle.)

Christmas Eve at Home. This typical scene shows Beth and Russell Waycott in their grandparents' home on Riverview Avenue in St. George in the late 1950s. Like most New Brunswickers, if there was a fireplace in the home, it was the place where stockings were hung. We see plastic creeping into Christmas in this "Merry Christmas" banner over the fireplace. (Courtesy of Elizabeth Toy.)

Spruce to Fir to Pine to Plastic. Spruce tips and spruce trees were preferred Victorian decorative material. Eventually spruce was replaced by fir, for it was discovered that fir kept its needles for a much longer time after being cut down. After the Second World War, pines began to interest the Christmas tree consumer. In this 1955 photo are three unidentified Saint Johners gathered around their pine tree. Today about a third of homes use a plastic tree. (Courtesy of Vintage Photo and Frame.)

Cards Filled in Many a Bare Spot! Glady MacLeod places some cards on her tree in her Saint John West home around 1960. By the 1950s the card exchange was at its height in New Brunswick, and many of the province's people found some seasonal employment as sorters or delivery personnel with the post office. However, gone were the days when one could post a card and expect it to be delivered on Christmas Day, as had been the case on Christmas Day in 1885, when the postmen delivered 5,094 cards. (Courtesy of Carol Whittaker.)

A Canadian Tradition Believed to Have Started in Saint John. One Saint John tradition that is believed to have spread and become a national event was the erection of a huge, lavishly decorated fir in the Charlotte Street branch of the Bank of Nova Scotia. This custom began after the bank was opened in 1939 and continues to this day. For more than forty years, the tree came from the same area of Hoyt. Saint John children would be taken to see the tree as part of their uptown visit to Santa a few blocks away at MRA's.

Christmas With the Troops. During World War II, Saint John Harbour was heavily guarded because it was a strategic shipping location for goods going overseas for the war effort. Men far from home still wanted to mark Christmas. These men belong to the Sergeant's Mess of the 8th Anti-Aircraft Battery and are pictured with their tree at the K Club Grounds in 1940. Left to right, they are Sgt. Elden Earl, Lt. Bob Kelly, Arizona Boudren, Sgt. C.W. Quinn, and Sgt. Len Walsh. (Courtesy of HW: Quinn Collection #2538.)

Not All Trees Looked This Good! We close this chapter with this 1900-era Saint John tree. Note the combination of homemade and store-bought decorations. Most photographs that have survived show that trees were usually wild looking, and the decorations were whatever the people could get their hands on. Today magazines that depict Victorian Christmas seem to think all trees of yesteryear looked like this one, which was probably professionally decorated for one of the wealthier families on Douglas Avenue. Perhaps among the printed cards on this tree is this popular Victorian greeting verse that is still appropriate to this day: "It's an old, old wish on a tiny little card./ It's simply 'Merry Christmas,' but I wish it very hard." (Courtesy of HW: Heritage Saint John #370.)

Five

Christmas in the Churches

Beautiful Decorative Effort, But Who Did It? The role of the church vis-a-vis Christmas changed greatly in the Victorian era. This comment from the *Fredericton Capital* of December 25, 1886, sums it up nicely: "Within the memory of men still young the observance of Christmas among English speaking people was confined to the Episcopal churches but a change has gradually crept on, now its recognition is the rule not the exception." This photo is from the collection of Christ Church Cathedral in Fredericton. Though it has appeared twice in the *New Brunswick Anglican*, there is still some question as to where this church stood. It may be St. Peter's at Head Line, near Welsford, a church deep in the wilderness that was closed in the 1950s when the army established Camp Gagetown. Perhaps with wider exposure, this will be confirmed, but for now, it serves simply as a well-decorated example of an Anglican church in the diocese of a century ago. (Courtesy of PA P36-25.)

Saint John's Oldest Church Building Always Well Decorated. St. George's Church has seen 175 Christmases come and go and since the late 1870s has been lavishly decorated for each of them. This view looks toward the altar; the picture below looks toward the rear of the church. The church newspaper, titled *Work* for January 1885, made this comment on the decorations: "A number of young people were busy for a week or more preparing decorations for the church." The *Saint John Globe* in December 1888 noted, "The decorations of St. George's Church cannot be surpassed if indeed they can be equalled," and the article went on to describe a sanctuary very similar to these pictures. (Courtesy of St. George's Church.)

St. George's Church.

Xmas Day   *1879*

Morning.

Hymn 60

Venite, ... Chant No. — *16*

Psalms 19.45.85 — *No - 2*

Te Deum, ... Chant No,

Benedictus, ... Chant No.

Hymn, *Carol VII* Tune No. *The Children*

Kyrie, ..., No.

Gloria, ... No.

Hymn, ... Tune No. *Carol 12*

Offertory Sentence — No. *Barnby / Gibbons*

Sanctus, ... No.

Gloria in Excelsis, No.

Evening.

Hymn 59 — *O come* . *Before Service*

Psalms, — *89* ... *St Augustine* — *16*

Magnificat, ... Chant No. *J Gilbert*

Nunc Dimittis, ... Chant No.

Anthem, *Carol , Carol Christians*

Hymn, *Earthly Friends Children +*

Hymn, ... Tune No.

A Lucky Find: an Xmas Service Sheet From 1879. This service sheet from St. George's Church has survived since 1879 because it was used as a receipt for the rector Theodore E. Dowling for his salary for the month of December 1878. The amount paid was $31.79. The hymns for Christmas Day, as identified from the hymnal in use at the time, *Hymns Ancient and Modern*, were "Hark! The Herald Angels Sing," "Of the Father's Love Begotten," and "O Come, All Ye Faithful." (Courtesy of St. George's Church archives.)

Choristers bring Xmas Greetings, 1900. St. George's Church had the only organ in Saint John West in the mid- to late-Victorian era, and the choir was well known for its musical presentations. Here at Christmas, 1900, is a card with the season's compliments from the choirboys written on the back. The choristers are, from left to right: (front row) Leonard Ougler, Powell Ougler, Joseph Maxwell, and George Peterson; (back row) Harry Hampton, Willy Sampson, Evan Peterson, Willie Maxwell, and Harold Ketchum. (Courtesy of St. George's Church archives.)

Exterior of St. George's about 1885. The choir shown in the top image was photographed against the west door and at the top of the steps leading into the nave of the church. This portion of the building has been tastefully preserved, much as it was in the Victorian era, and St. George's is decorated extensively to this day, although plastic greenery is used instead of spruce due to fire regulations. (Courtesy of St. George's Church archives.)

Decorated Rood Screen of the Mother Church of Anglicism in Saint John. Trinity Church in the centre of Saint John was built to be the cathedral church of the Anglicans of the province following the great fire of 1877 in Saint John. This is the same year when residents of the biggest city still hoped the capital in Fredericton would be moved back to its original home in Saint John. The Trinity Church was the first church where New Brunswickers heard the entire *Messiah* with a full orchestra in the year 1885. Then as now, it was decorated with live greens for the performance. When vestments were introduced for the 60-voice choir at Easter in 1890, it was not popular with all church members. (Courtesy of Geoff Foss.)

Miss Knights's Sunday School Scholars at Trinity Church. Sunday school students were treated to a party each Christmas following December 25th. Santa was the chief attraction, and he would always unveil a tree bedecked with presents. The children would rush the tree and plunder the gifts. Sometimes Santa got knocked onto his backside, and once, at the Fairville Methodist Church in Saint John West, he caught fire after being pushed into the candles on the tree. (Courtesy of Geoff Foss.)

Vested Boys Choir at Trinity about 1910. A Saint John report of December 28, 1887, noted: "'Christmas Cantata,' 'Santa Claus Mistake,' or the 'Bundle of Sticks' by St. David Church's young scholars at the Sunday school. Little operettas, pretty music, dances, choruses." In the case of the above photo, most of Trinity's organists were emigrants from England, so its natural that the choir was dressed in the English tradition and featured boys only, for it was the norm in English cathedrals where the organists trained. (Courtesy of Geoff Foss.)

A Turn-of-the-Century Teacher's Greeting. Mechanisation of the printing process with the resulting reduction in costs combined with the ability to produce colour more cheaply made it possibly for churches to procure greeting cards for the season, such as this one from Jessie Stafford, teacher of class #7, at the Marysville Free Baptist Church outside Fredericton. This would have cost the teacher about 25¢ each.

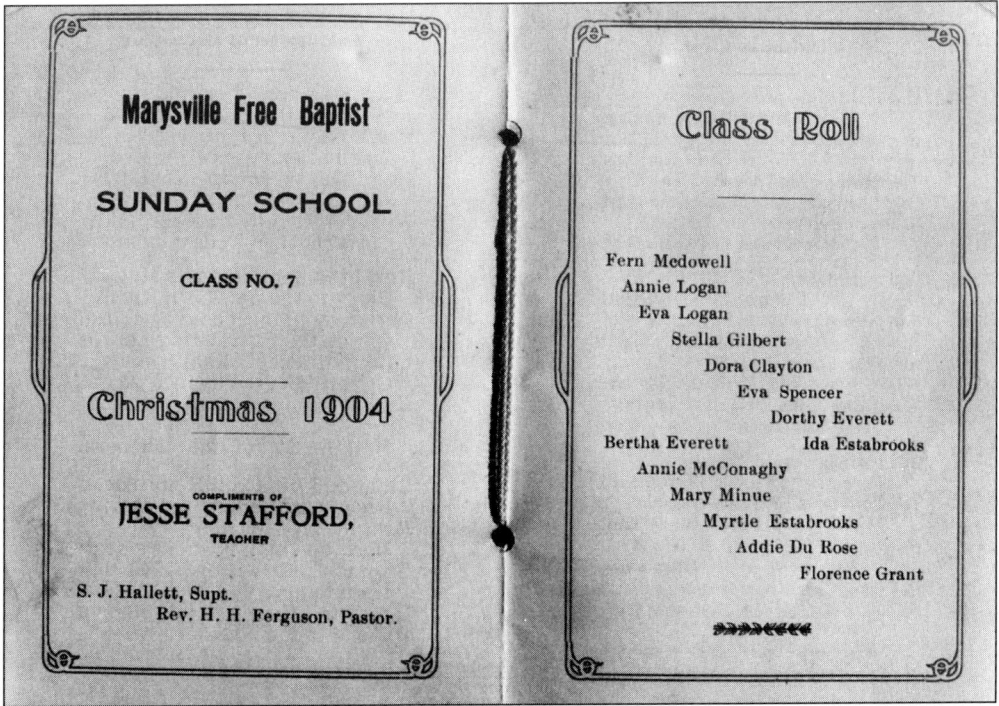

Marysville Free Baptist

SUNDAY SCHOOL

CLASS NO. 7

Christmas 1904

COMPLIMENTS OF
JESSE STAFFORD,
TEACHER

S. J. Hallett, Supt.
Rev. H. H. Ferguson, Pastor.

Class Roll

Fern Mcdowell
Annie Logan
Eva Logan
Stella Gilbert
Dora Clayton
Eva Spencer
Dorthy Everett
Bertha Everett   Ida Estabrooks
Annie McConaghy
Mary Minue
Myrtle Estabrooks
Addie Du Rose
Florence Grant

Caraquet Alter Featured on Postcard. The Roman Catholic population of New Brunswick (and this includes the Acadians of the east and north shore) did not go for lavish decoration in their churches. The *Saint John Globe* in December 1888 noted: "At the Cathedral on Waterloo Street little decoration disturbed the solemn appearance of the building with only a few greens placed on the altar."

Gathering for Church in St. Leonard. This photo from the St. Leonard Historical Society gives no indication of the occasion but serves to show the transition from the earliest era when everyone walked to church to the age of the automobile. There is still a holdout to the old days, such as the sleigh near the barn to the right of the weathered church. One of the most precious memories of the Catholic and especially Acadian Catholic families is the midnight mass and the "Reveillon," or the food feast that followed late into the night. The children in Acadian areas did not expect much for Christmas, but some did hang their stockings and receive an orange, some hard candy, and a small toy. (Courtesy of PA P 51-194.)

Two Creche to Consider. One element of the Roman Catholic Christmas that did not become fashionable in the Protestant circles until after World War II was the Creche. At old St. Peter's behind Fort Howe in Saint John, the *Globe* newspaper noted: "The representation of the stable in Bethlehem to the left of the main entrance showing the Godchild in the manger altar is a very tasteful piece of work and reflects great credit upon the brother having charge of the sanctuary." (Top picture courtesy of HW: Joe Michaud, Heritage Saint John.)

When the Cathedral of the Immaculate Conception opened its doors on Christmas Day in 1855 in Saint John, the working class Irish immigrants that were its main adherents were so glad to have a church to worship in that three thousand showed up with candles in the unheated and unlit building for the 6:00 am Mass. (Bottom picture courtesy of PA P20-166.)

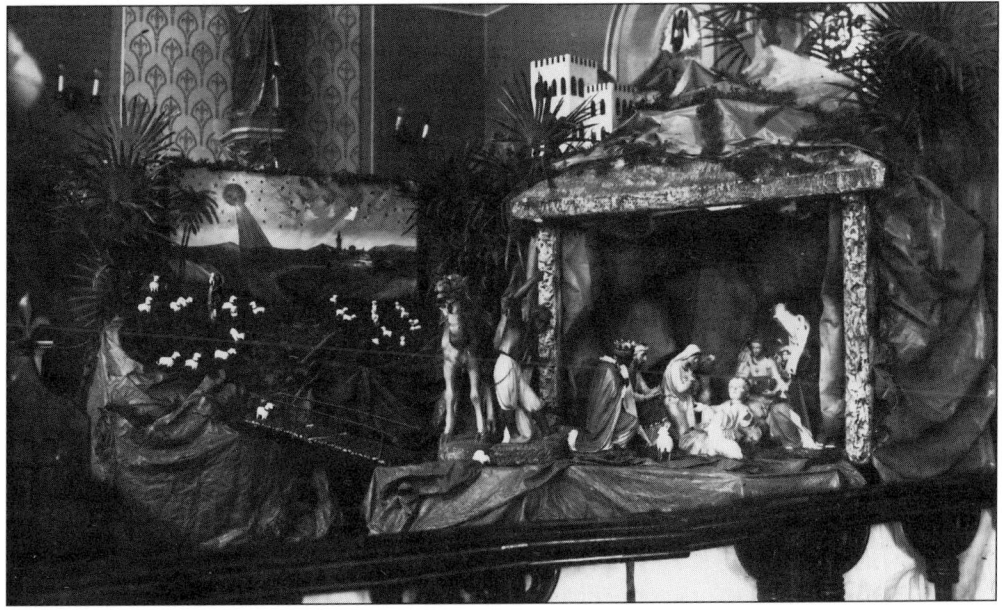

Choir Procession in Bathurst. The Nicholas Denys Historical Society gives us another glimpse of the Acadian, or north shore, church with the choirboys and alter boys lined up for service in a church identified only as Bathurst Ouest. With the services still spoken in Latin, the Catholic-Acadian knowledge of the carols popular in the Victorian era was not extensive. While the English enjoyed many carols, the Catholics shared only "O Come, All Ye Faithful" and "Silent Night" with the Protestant churchgoers. In the Catholic church, it was more likely that there would be a presentation of Mozart's Twelfth Mass, Farmer's Mass in B-flat, or F.X. Schmidt's Mass in E-flat than a carol sing. (Courtesy of PA P 20-168.)

Saint Mary's Church in Saint John. This church stood at the foot of the Waterloo Street hill. When this photo was taken around 1900, the Reverend W.O. Raymond, one of the leading historians in New Brunswick, was the rector of the church. He served from 1884–1916 and made sure it was always tastefully decorated. One of the works begun under his rectorship was the formation of a church band, which is still active as St. Mary's (Community) Band, though the church was torn down in 1971. (Courtesy of Vintage Photo and Frame #9042.)

Christmas Preparations for the Poor. On the Sunday before Christmas, 1909, the adherents of Centenary Church in Saint John had a summary of their efforts displayed in their church hall for all to admire. With the exception of the tins and the doll, all are wrapped in white, a tradition that started in the Methodist Episcopal church in Ohio in 1904 and spread quickly to Maritime churches. This church was built to accommodate fifteen hundred; however, the statistics displayed on this board indicate a smaller congregation. Still, good works were an important part of the mission then and now. (Courtesy of Vintage Photo and Frame #9722.)

The Sunday School Hall of Centenary Church in 1909. Teachers and scholars are gathered around a 20-foot fir tree and surrounded by their efforts to meet the need of the home and foreign missions. Centenary's work in this regard was typical of the churches in Saint John, which was called a "Saintly city indeed!" by an American visitor when told the city had thirty-three churches and four missions to serve 41,000 people. These decorations would have been put up before Christmas for the bazaar or fancy sale. One described on December 8, 1879, for

Centenary said, "Tea meeting and sale will be held in the parlour of Centenary Church. Good assortment of useful articles, Christmas table, beautiful wax works by Mrs. Narraway, tea from 6 to 8 pm, admission 10 cents, tickets for tea, 30 cents." Following Christmas, the same decorations would be used at the supper for the poor of the area and a few days later, the annual visit of Santa Claus to the Sunday schoolchildren. (Courtesy of Vintage Photo and Frame.)

Christmas Pageant Time in New York. Alice Huige and Susan Scott were two of several thousand children who donned wings and fitted haloes to play angels in the telling of the Christmas story. As ministers became more and more disillusioned with the merchandising of Santa and his intrusion into Sunday school programs, they began plays, tableaus, pageants, readings, and recitations in the churches and Sunday schools as a way of conveying the story of the birth of Jesus. The plays came almost entirely from American publishing houses who used works by men like Henry Van Dyke's *The Other Wise Man*, Martha Race's *Why the Chimes Rang*, or Lyman Bayard's *When the Stars Shone*. These photos are of Alice Huige's New York City church, where she was part of the pageants, which bore great similarity to ones held in New Brunswick churches. (Courtesy of Alice Huige.)

ST. GEORGE'S FAIR

November, 27th. and 28th.
Tuesday Evening 7 p. m.
Thursday 4 to 10 p. m.

ADMISSION 10C.

Christmas Gifts you'll find, for one and all, for Santa has left them at St. George's Hall. November twenty-seven at seven o'clock, our Shoppes will open just on the dot. We'll continue next day, beginning at four, and we'll keep it up till ten or more. Our Shoppes are many' our Goods are new, if you cannot buy them, at least come to view.

The first on the list is the "Snow-ball Tree"-then "Kris Kringle Kandy Shoppe" you will see. For bargains of which, we all want some, try "Cash and Carry" and back you'll come. At the "Needle Work Shoope" are bargains more, and the "Handkerchief Shoppe" is right next door.

There's "Iceland" too, where of course you must go, you won't find it cold tho there'll be lots of snow.

St. George's Cooks are at the top,-so patronize the "Cookery Shoppe". In the Hall you'll find a "Post Office" too - a parcel may there be addressed to you. The Tiny Wee Tots you mustn't forget, but at "Dolly Dingles" their wants will be met. "Frozen Goodness" of course you'll have to eat and the "Cover Up Shoppe" it can't be beat. French Cooks will serve you with "Kringles" rare and so ends the Shoppes at St. George's Fair,

Clever Promotion to Catch the Patron's Attention. There was hardly a church in the cities or towns at the turn of the century who didn't have a similar promotion like St. George's Church. Proceeds from three or four days of work at such bazaars or fairs would net around $200. The average Anglican church in the province of New Brunswick in 1896 operated on an annual budget of $1,150, so the bazaars covered a considerably portion of the year's needs from a secular Christmas activity. A comment by Rev R.W. Colston of the church at Douglas Harbour at Grand Lake in 1896 is quite telling: "Though many profess to being warm friends of the church, yet their warmth has not yet penetrated as far as their pocketbook." (Courtesy of St. George's Church archives.)

Salvation Army Bandsmen Ready For the Carolling Season. The Salvation Army is truly a church of the Victorian era; it had spread to every province of Canada by 1886. In 1890 in Fredericton, bandsmen were asked to give up their "drumming and screeching nuisance and outlandish noise" after a colt driven by Charles Orr was so frightened by the bandsmen that it bolted, fell, and got badly cut. A petition was taken to council, but the bandsmen toned down the approach, and the good work of the Army soon won over the residents. (Courtesy of Salvation Army, George Scott Railton Heritage Centre.)

Another Victorian Idea: the Familiar Christmas Kettle Campaign. This tradition had its beginning on the streets of San Francisco in 1891 when the No. 4 Corp found itself short of funds to feed a thousand needy people at Christmas. It was the idea of Joseph McPhee, who had been a sailor in England and was familiar with this custom in Liverpool, to put out an iron pot, called Simpson's Pot, which had been placed on the Liverpool wharves so those passing by could drop in coins for needy seamen. In 1995 in Canada, 11,619 volunteers manned the kettles, and those passing by tossed in some 4.9 million in coins. (Courtesy of Salvation Army, George Scott Railton Heritage Centre.)

Six

The Schools at Christmas

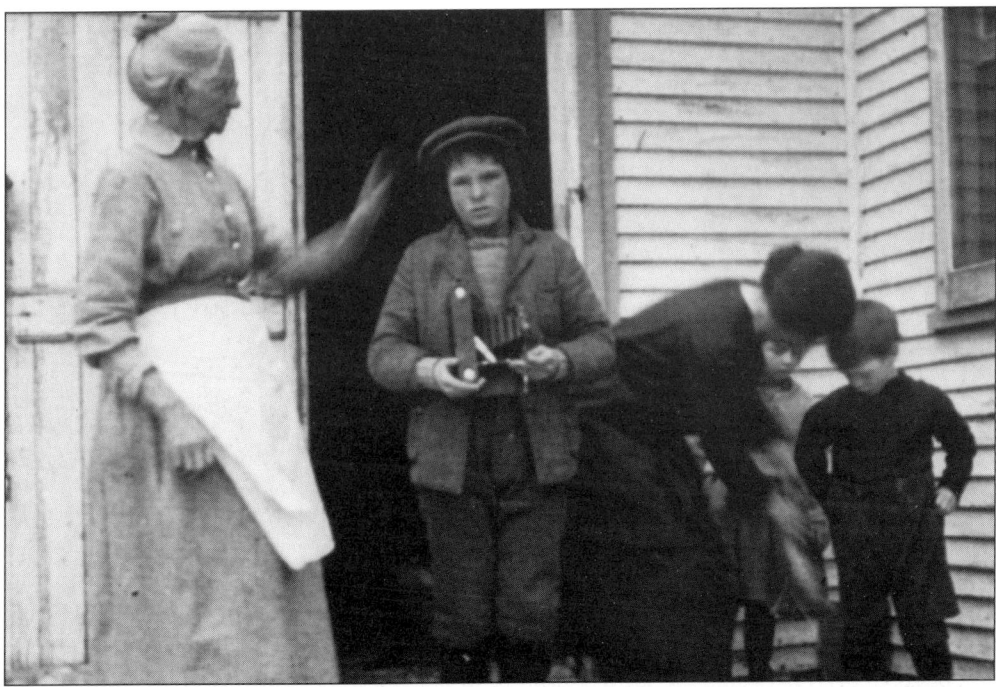

A Presentation at the Maces Bay Schoolhouse. Representative of the scene at many a Christmas closing was the presentation of a camera to a student. In this 1921 photograph, Milton Shaw was awarded this gift for his good work in the schoolhouse. Until the equal opportunity programs of 1967, when one-room schoolhouses with their multiple classes started to disappear, the children of the province celebrated the coming of Christmas as a family might—a family-like mix of young and old with a variety of talents to share at the end of the fall term. When the superintendent or his/her staff made a visit to test the children and to test that their teacher was doing his/her job, the superintendent would often bring a quiz as a challenge to the children. (Courtesy of Victor Duffy.)

Gibson School, York County, Decorated For the Season. The Gibson School was located on the north side of Fredericton and took its name from industrialist Alexander Gibson of Marysville. There was a connection between the business world and the schools in earlier times as there is today; the *Daily Telegraph* wrote on December 23, 1892, that "a large number of prizes of books, boxes, and skates were awarded [to] successful competitors of the closing examinations." (Courtesy of PA P 61-443.)

North Carleton County Schools, 1940s. Children have their own desks in this photo, unlike those at the Gibson School. Many country scholars have memories of dramatic presentations during the evenings just before Christmas. On these occasions desks would be pushed back, chairs set up, and parents, grandparents, and neighbours would fill them for an evening show. A makeshift stage would be at the front of the room, and the students would do their first public singing, elocution, or playing of a musical instrument. It was an experience that stood them in good stead for the rest of their lives. (Courtesy of PA P 26-2.)

A mid-1950s Photo of the North Carleton County School. In this classroom is a full-size tree and a chalkboard Santa as decorative elements for the parents attending a closing, which by the 1950s, was an afternoon affair in many schools. By this time, the antics of Rudolph, the invention of Robert L. May at the beginning of World War II, were becoming popular and Frosty and Suzie Snowflake were replacing old-time recitations. (Courtesy of PA P 26-17.)

An Island Schoolroom in Saint John Harbour. Partridge Island has served as the city's quarantine station from the time of the Irish immigrants (1847) and was pressed into service as a military base during World War I. Following the war, lightkeepers and hospital workers stayed on the island and their children were schooled there. This is Miss Jean MacCallum, their teacher, who was playing Santa in this 1923 photo. Others in the picture are Ruby Prosser, Charlie Cochrane, Bernice Prosser, and Alan and Margaret Hargrove, who are all grouped around Santa. (Courtesy of HW: Hargrove collection PIRP 50-34.)

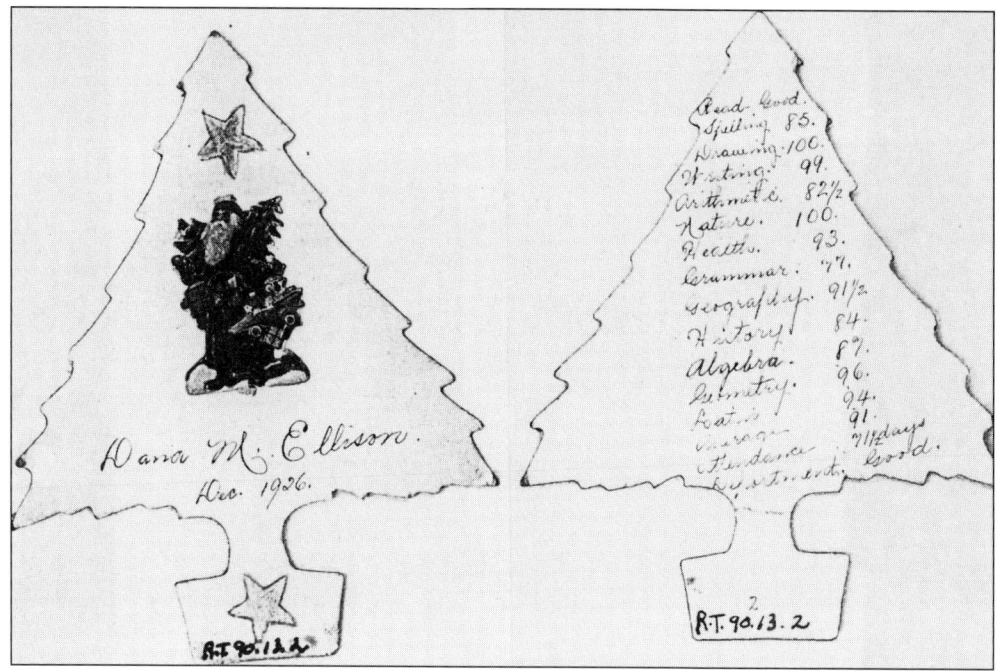

Teachers Had to Be Innovative. To encourage students and stretch resources in times past, teachers often used ingenious ways to challenge and reward students. To conclude the Christmas term, this teacher used a tree-shaped piece of construction paper for the report card, and on both sides added comments and the student's marks. It has been separated only to show both sides. (Courtesy of the School Days Museum, Fredericton.)

Nativity at Netherwood. The presentation of the Nativity is not encouraged today in the New Brunswick school system. In private schools, though, the time-honoured Gospel story is still part of the Christmas closing. Netherwood School for Girls has been merged with the Rothesay Collegiate for Boys; however, this building no longer exists. The girls who presented this drama in 1955 have carried the memory of a New Brunswick Christmas to all parts of the world, for they have gone on to careers in many far-flung places. (Courtesy of PA P 198-17.)

Seven
Christmas Amusements

Two Pillars of Victorian Entertainment. Standing side by side on Carleton Street in Saint John were the Mechanics Institute (on the left), opened in 1840 and a representative of the secular side of Christmas, and the Stone Church (on the right), officially St. Mark's, dating from 1824 and a representative of the sacred. Both these institutions survived the calamitous 1877 fire that destroyed central Saint John. The Mechanics Institute, though, did not survive the ravages of time. It became the Nickel Theatre in 1907 and burned down in 1913. In this chapter we shall see various forms of entertainment as captured by photographers around the province.

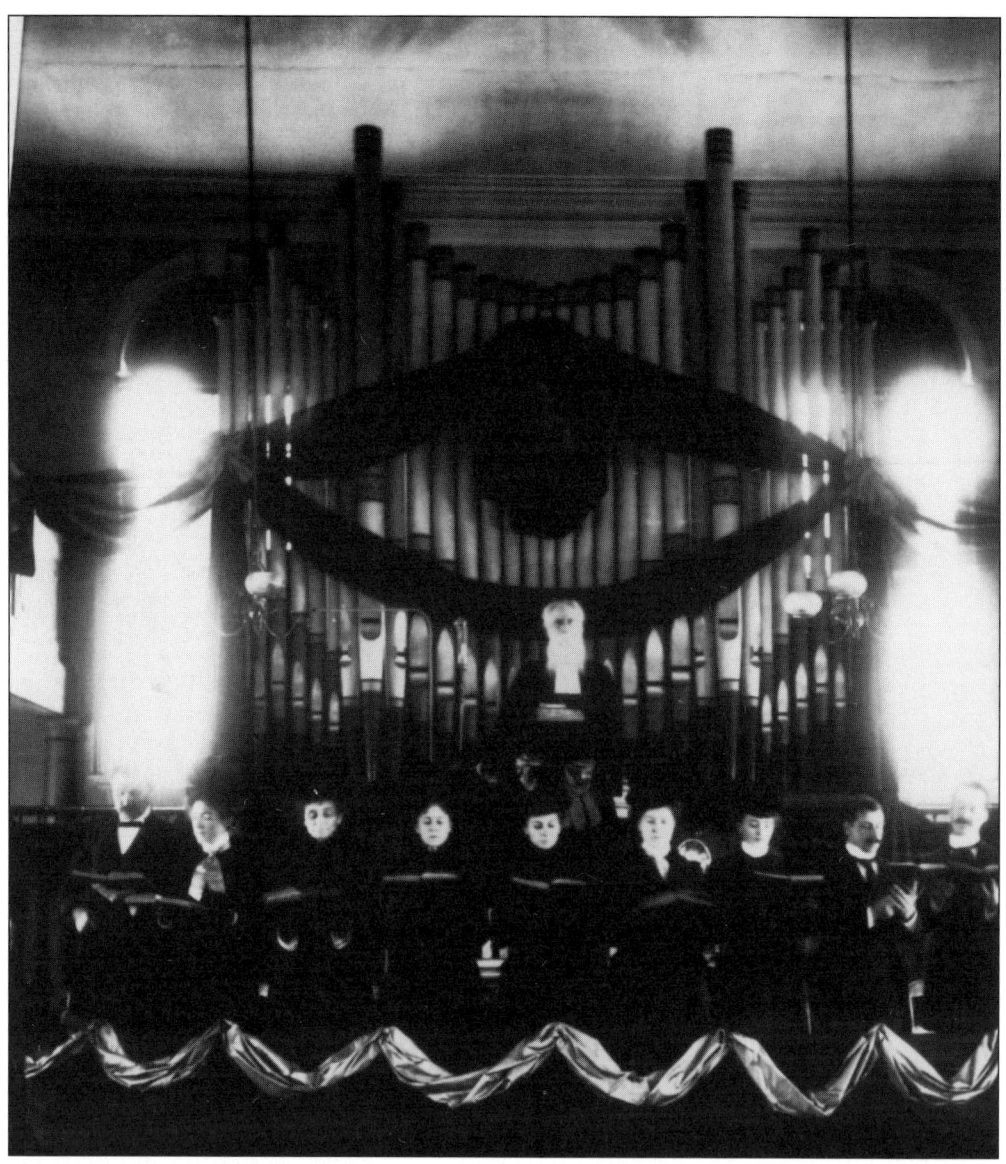

St. James Choristers Marking the Death of Victoria. Church choirs all over the province prepared special music for Christmas and other notable occasions. In 1896 the choir of Stone Church, seen on the previous page, sang Vincent's "There Were Shepherds" along with the proper responses and "The Magnificat" and "Nunc Dimittis." No doubt the choir of Saint James Church in Newcastle, pictured here with the Father of the Lord Beaverbrook in the centre, did likewise, though on this occasion, they were lamenting the death of the monarch whose love of Christmas was instrumental in its shape to this day. (Courtesy of PA P 62.)

There Were Secular Choruses, Too. Though we have the idea that they sang door to door during the Victorian period, the newspapers and diaries used in research for this book gave no evidence for this case. Rather, we know these choral groups hired halls and did presentations to augment school, church, and home entertainments. The photo above shows the St. George Choral group, which performed in December of 1890. It was probably taken following a presentation in the town's Broadway Theatre by photographer E.R. O'Brien, the grandmother of Elizabeth Toy. Below are the players of a three-act play on the same occasion; from left to right are: (standing) Mae Epps, George O'Dow, Edna O'Brien, unidentified, Heloise (Gilmore) MacKenzie, Stewart MacAdam, Georgie (Patterson) Dow, Morton L. Kennedy, Ken Campbell, and Otty Kennedy; (seated) unidentified, unidentified, Mrs. Hugh Laurence, Wes Spinney, Mrs. Laura Goss, Pheobe L. Toy, and May McIntyre. (Courtesy of Elizabeth Toy.)

To the Theatre. The birth of theatre can be traced back to February 1789, when *The Busybody* and *Whose the Dupe* played at the Mallard House in Saint John. In 1867 Dickens was invited to come to Saint John while on a North American tour. He was so worn out after dramatising *The Christmas Carol* across the continent that he did not make it to the city; impersonators of Dickens did, however, and they drew great crowds. The group pictured here presented the program on page 77 at Hartland on December 25, 1914. The photo was taken by Percy Wentzell. From left to right are Stan Keays, Curtis Simms, Kenneth Keith, Ray Plummer, and Orrin Hovey.

In this picture are: (front row) Stan Keays; (second row) Anna Murdock, Elsa Sipprelle, Kenneth Keith, Helen Aiton, and Ray Plummer; (back row) Curtis Simms, Tress Alton, Clara Hagerman, Orrin Hovey, and Mary Carr. (Courtesy of Doris Kennedy.)

(handwritten annotations) St. Paul's "Foresters Hall" 1916 & 1917
(handwritten, vertical left margin) Mr. Harry Gillin played Piano &

PATRIOTIC
ENTERTAINMENT

HARTLAND
XMAS NIGHT, - - - 1914

By Hartland Amateurs in Aid of Canadian Patriotic and Belgian Relief Funds presenting

"A Rival by Request"

A Comedy in three acts

CAST

WALTER PIERSON—young bachelor — Ken' Keith
WINTHROP SMYTHE his friend — *~~Geo. Boyer~~* *(handwritten)*
ROBT. BURNETT—retired business man — ~~L. Marathon~~ *(handwritten)* Stan Kaye
BENJ. BRIGGS—retired farmer *(handwritten)* Amen Hovey • ~~W. Hovey~~
LORD ALBERT McMULLIN—friend of Smythe's — P. A. Wentzell *(handwritten)*
ALEX MUGGINS—Smythe's servant — Ray Plummer
MRS. BURNETT—wife of Robert — Miss A. Murdock
MARGARET BURNETT—her daughter — Miss H. Aiton
MRS. BRIGGS—wife of Benjamin — Miss M. Carr
ELIZA BRIGGS—her daughter — Miss E. Sipprell
MRS. CHATTERTON—housekeeper, Cosmopole, Miss C. Hagerman

SCENES I and II — Pierson's Apartment at the "Cosmopole".
SCENE III—At the "St George."

PATRIOTIC SONGS AND OTHER SPECIALTIES
"GOD SAVE THE KING"

Observer Print *(handwritten)* Elmer Alexander • Pin

Bandsmen Touring by Sleigh at Chatham. The presence of bands at bazaars, entertainments, and banquets and their public presentations are referred to again and again in newspaper accounts in the late Victorian era. For example, "#4 Bryson's Band with a long string of sleighs formed a quite impressive sight as they drove through the city," reported the *Fredericton Capital* in 1870. A few years later, on January 1, 1887, the *Gleaner* reported, "Marysville Brass Band, in a monster sleigh, crossed the river and passed through most of the streets." Here St. Michael's Band is out for an afternoon of merry-making in Chatham. (Courtesy of the J.C.Y. Mersereau collection PA P 18-34.)

St. Michael's Band Again—This Time on Foot. Outside concerts were not an isolated event as this second picture of St. Michael's Band of Chatham shows. They were especially active as agents of the Roman Catholic Total Abstinence Society and were busiest on St. Patrick's Day, when the band would play on the streets of Chatham from morning to evening. The *Maramichi Advance* on January 31, 1889, reports that this band showed up to play a serenade for Mr. Thomas Fitzpatrick and his bride, who had just been married at the Pro Cathedral, perhaps after a Christmas social brought them together. (Courtesy of PA P 6-299.)

A.V.F. Duffy with his Christmas Accordion, 1916. A.V.F. Duffy would have had a huge variety of party pieces to choose from and wouldn't have necessarily played carols, but would have relied on waltzes, Irish tunes and others popular pieces still known today, such as "When You Were Sweet 16," Sullivan's "The Lost Chord," "The Spider and the Fly," or "My Wild Irish Rose" from Willer's Instructional Booklets. (Courtesy of Victor Duffy.)

Louise and Ruth Knight Enjoying a Reading Session, 1910. The ladies might be enjoying Dickens or Washington Irving or even a New Brunswick writer, such as Charles G.D. Roberts, whose animal stories were popular. Perhaps the Christmas sections from *Little Women*, the words of Henry Van Dyke, or the reading of *The Cricket on the Hearth*, which was the most popular of Dickens's work performed on the stage in Saint John, would entice a reader. (Courtesy of Geoff Foss.)

Eight
Santa's Development and Role

Though a Fredericton merchant, Charles Sampson had Santa delivering gifts in the early 1870s, and some New Brunswick children no doubt knew of illustrations of Santa from Clement Moore's "A Visit from St. Nicholas," or Thomas Nast's cartoons in *Harper's Weekly*. However, Santa's appearance was still mysterious to most. Provincial papers began carrying images of him in the early 1880s, and soon after, he began to appear regularly at Sunday school parties, school closings, etc. About 1890, he began appearing at Manchester, Roberston Allison's big King Street store in Saint John, and he later held court in Scovil's Oak Hall, also on King Street. Santa was still quite a novelty in the first decade of this century. In 1909, when the Nickel Theatre on Carleton Street in Saint John announced that "pudgy little Santa Claus himself" would come out of a fireplace onto their stage (as shown on this page) at 3:15 and 3:45 each day of the week before Christmas for the Kriss Kringle Matinee, the *Daily Sun* reported that a thousand children showed up, and the show was the "talk of the town." The *Sun* noted, "little ones tittered and jumped with delight" upon seeing Santa. (Courtesy Vintage Photo and Frame #9983.)

Two Peeks at Pre-photo Santa. This wood-cut (above) in the *Fredericton Capital* of December 23, 1882, is very much like the images that appeared in the very first illustration of the "Visit of St. Nicholas" when Clement Moore, a man of the cloth, finally admitted he wrote the piece and allowed it to be printed in 1848. To the left is a wild-looking, roly-poly Santa as depicted by an artist for the *Moncton Transcript* on December 24, 1889.

Santa in the Window of Oak Hall. This 1909 photo is the earliest one found while putting this book together. His appearance is not unlike that of the "Nickel" Santa on page 81. At Scovil's, Santa passed out pieces of chocolate, lollipops, and peppermint sticks to those who visited the Oak Hall store. In 1928 Santa's appearance on a Saturday morning was still rare enough that 3,500 kids lined up to see him. Before 1950, those who wanted a picture of Santa brought a camera along. After that, MRA's made it into a commercial operation and took the picture for a fee. (See close up of this Santa on page 4.) (Courtesy of Vintage Photo and Frame.)

The Nickel Theatre Kriss Kringle Matinee. Santa comes to the stage of the Nickel Theatre on Carleton Street via the fireplace. The Nickel was successor to the Mechanic's Institute (shown on page 73). This photo was taken in 1910, three years before the theatre burned to the ground. (Courtesy of Vintage Photo and Frame.)

Santa at MRA's with Brenda Seeley in 1950. This was a popular tradition that most Saint John families shared in the boom days following the war. These faded and cracked photos are now childhood treasures of the baby boomers.

Santa with Carl and Bob Tilley in 1955 at MRA's. Santa is seen at every mall today, but when Carl and Bob Tilley visited the store in the 1955, Jimmy McEachern was the only Santa in town!

Santa in 1953 with Carol (Oliver) Whittaker. Children from the New Brunswick Protestant Orphanage Home (see chapter 12) were also taken to see MRA's Santa—and the little secrets they whispered often came true as will be seen on pages 119–121.

Santa Was Busy at Sunday School Parties, Too. Santa was also busy visiting church groups in the 1950s. Movies shown via 35mm projectors had became the favourite form of entertaining children at Sunday school parties, replacing the recitations that were the favoured entertainment of earlier years. Fortunately another custom, rushing to get wrapped gifts and candy tied to the tree, called stripping the tree, had faded too. This photo is of St. Anthony's Church in Devon, near Fredericton. (Courtesy of PA P 163-77.)

Santa's Image Is Defined. In the 1950s Santa's image was standardized and illustrations weren't much different than photos of Santa. This is the first Santa Claus parade in Saint John of November 19, 1951. By the early 1950s, the stores in Saint John, Fredericton, and Moncton kept later hours in the weeks leading up to Christmas instead of remaining open only on Christmas Eve. (Courtesy of Vintage Photo and Frame.)

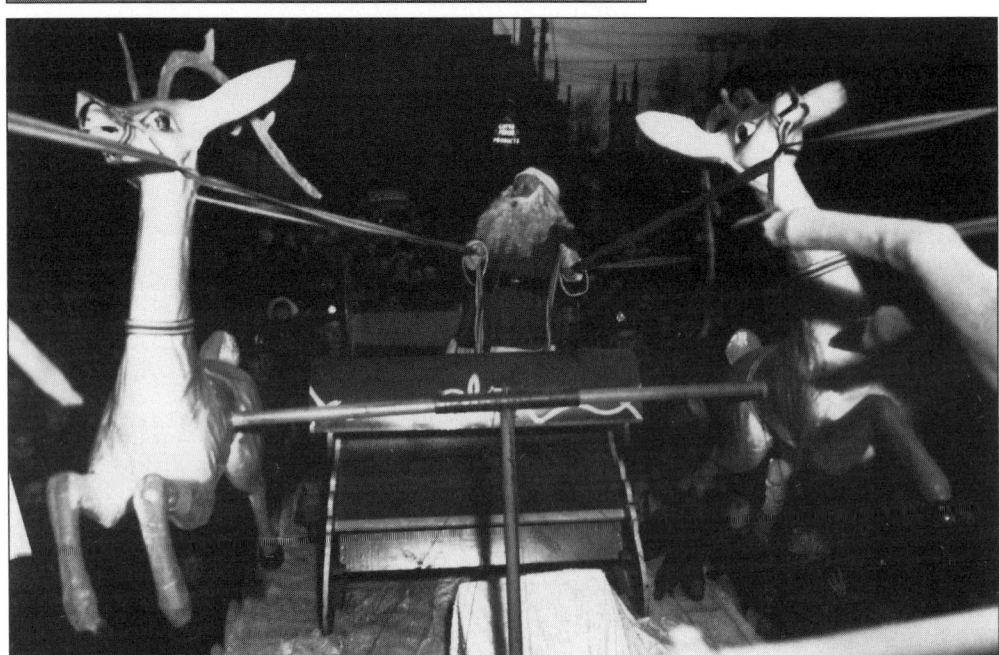

Santa Is Paraded through Saint John. Joe Michaud took this photo of Santa pulling up to the "lower-price" floor of MRA's on Germain Street on November 19, 1951. This was forty-nine years after Eaton's had staged Canada's first parade in Toronto. The early parades began at the Armouries on City Road, went around Haymarket Square, up the steep hill of Waterloo Street, along King Square North to Charlotte, and down King Street. Sometimes, Santa would climb up a ladder into MRA's second floor toyland. (Courtesy of Vintage Photo and Frame.)

Santa Brings Up the Rear of the Parade. No matter how many entries, the Santa float was always at the end of the parade. Here it travels up Prince Edward Street past the tenements of the area. Ed Murphy had the job of arranging the parade from 1954 to the last MRA's-sponsored parade in 1972. He began preparations in October. The papier-mache reindeer often required extensive work. Jimmy MacEachern, the store porter who played Santa, insisted on the best yak beard for authenticity. As a result, Mr. Murphy recalls the budget was often overshot. (Courtesy of Vintage Photo and Frame.)

Grimm's Fairy Tales or Nursery Rhymes Parade Themes. The "little old lady who lived in a shoe" is shown on Charlotte Street in front of the F.W. Woolworth store. Though people didn't know it at the time, national chains like Woolworth's, located uptown, and Sears, located in the city's first strip mall at Fairview Plaza, were the beginning of the end of MRA's dominance in Saint John. (Courtesy of Vintage Photo and Frame.)

King Street, Saint John, as the Parade Concludes. Thousands turned out for the Saturday morning parade sponsored by MRA's, as can be seen in this parade photo of November 14, 1953. For Ed Murphy and his crew, the busy Christmas season would just be starting in the MRA store. They put up big archways of greenery on the Germain Street side and filled the seven front windows on King Street with imaginative displays. They had some 4 acres in all to decorate. Toyland, of course, got the most attention. The Santa Claus parade is still held in Saint John with the support of merchants and citizens and will soon celebrate its 50th anniversary. (Courtesy of Vintage Photo and Frame.)

Santa Comes to a Company Town. The MacLeans in Blacks Harbour, owners of Connor's Brothers, felt the same seasonal benevolence as the owners of MRA's and also arranged a visit from Santa on his sleigh. Santa continues to visit the town on Christmas Eve to pass out gifts and treats. This sleigh has only six reindeer, but unlike the Saint John float, it had a lead reindeer named Rudolph for this December 21, 1956 photo. (Courtesy of Elizabeth Toy.)

Nine

The Shops

In the 1860s merchants began decorating with greens and placing advertising space in newspapers, whose writers then added glowing commentary about the stores to their columns. Not all newsmen agreed with this procedure. On December 20, 1884, one wrote: "The scribe is expected to tell all that is for sale and a little more . . . to scatter taffy promiscuously on the hardware establishment and the vendor of two cent knickknacks, and to lay the blarney on with a skill of a lover." This St. Stephen store is stocked for Christmas with choice cigars with wrappers expressing good wishes. (Courtesy PA P 128-104.)

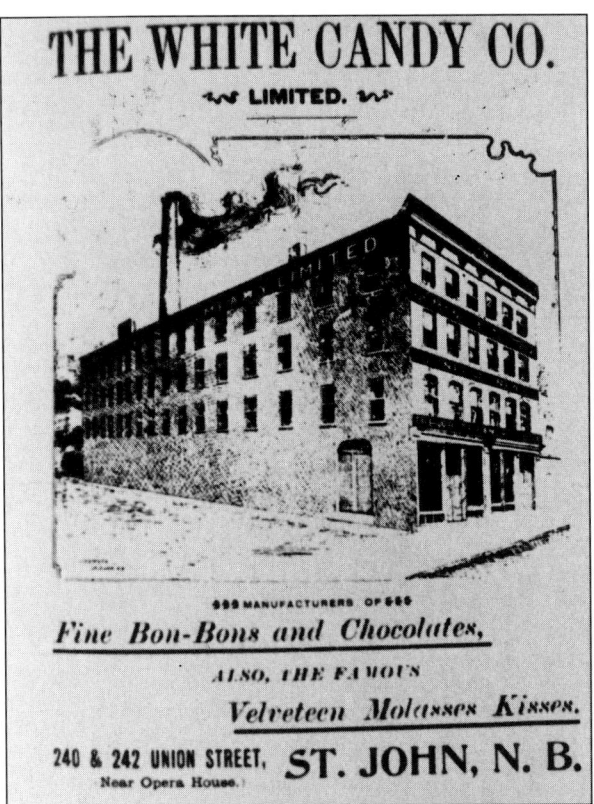

THE WHITE CANDY CO.

LIMITED.

Fine Bon-Bons and Chocolates,

ALSO, THE FAMOUS

Velreteen Molasses Kisses.

240 & 242 UNION STREET, **ST. JOHN, N. B.**
Near Opera House.

Sweet Tooth Satisfied Locally. The Frank White Candy Company in Saint John operated on Union Street and was also the concessioner of the Rockwood Park-Lily Lake Pavilion (seen in the postcard on page 26), where they sold their candy and sandwiches and ice cream. Chocolate cream drops, chocolate mice, cinnamon sticks, gum drops, rock candy, and lemon, orange, and licorice sticks were some of the favoured White products.

Saint John's Top Retail Location. F.W. Daniel and Company stood at the "Head of King," Saint Johners' nickname for the top of King Street where it meets Charlotte Street. This is arguably the best store location in the city and a site later taken over by Woolworths. Daniel's store was favoured by the ladies as the place to buy the latest fashions.

Charlie Parker's Bazaar, Henry Street, Newcastle. The church or club bazaar was the alternative to the commercial shops. It mattered little where they were because if they put up a tree and decorated a hall, people would travel for miles to attend these sales and purchase the handmade goods as alternatives to commercial products. One example from the south of the province is at Ossekeag, now known as Hampton, when a church advertised an "Xmas sale" on Tuesday, December 18, 1867; a special train was put on from Saint John. It cost 70¢ for the return trip, yet the train was filled. (Courtesy PA P 6-101.)

Remember the Five and Dime Stores? Refresh Your Memory! The Federal Stores (Phone 3-3168) operated a variety shop at 11–15 Charlotte Street in uptown Saint John. At first, business was so good that it expanded into an "L" shape store and wrapped around the corner building and had a second entrance at 160 Union Street. S.R. Taylor was the first manager in 1939, and Lorne W. MacKay was the manager when it closed in 1957. Its chief competitors

were Woolworths, the Met, and Zellers. All three chains opened or expanded stores in the uptown in the years the Federal Stores operated. The development of suburban malls eventually put all the five-and-dime-type stores in the uptown out of business. (Courtesy of Vintage Photo and Frame.)

Fredericton Retailers Filled Christmas Needs. Fancy Vermont turkeys in the range of 21–23 pounds hang in the butcher shop of V.E. Miller around 1900. They would have sold for 11–12¢ a pound. Chicken went for 30–40¢ and goose was 70–80¢ a pound. Besides the established merchants, there was a lively farmer's market in the city, and sometimes fifty teams would be selling. In 1889 the *Gleaner* reported, "In Phoenix Square there was hardly room for all the teams and a number took up positions away back on the hill while others occupied the gutters." (Courtesy of PA P 32-74.)

Fresh Fruit From the Sunny South. Citrus fruit in the Victorian era was brought into the Maritimes by ice pack boxcars. It took about a week to travel by rail from the sunny South. Merchants carried raisins, valencia oranges, lemons, apples, bananas, figs, dates, and all the necessary supplies for fruit cake and plum pudding. (Courtesy of PA P 32-73.)

V.E. Miller Sold the Symbol of Friendship. The pineapple, long a symbol of friendship, was a popular decorative motif in the past as it is now. It was available at V.E. Miller a century ago. Merchants, such as Miller, competed vigorously to decorate their shops attractively. Said the *Gleaner* in 1889: "Fredericton has taken on a festive appearance and the principal streets bear comparison with the best streets in cities of much greater size." (Courtesy of PA P 32-110.)

Look at the Staff—You Don't See That Today! Nine butchers stand ready to assist the Christmas shopper at V.E. Miller's Fredericton shop. There is no doubt that the turkey was the favourite Christmas treat. As early as December 24, 1831, the *New Brunswick Courier* published a poem that indicates this; it read: "Lay the proud old turkeys low. Let the young ones run and grow./ To market they're not fit to go . . . till next Christmas Day." (Courtesy of PA P 32-75.)

Books to Expand the Mind. Books were popular Christmas gifts a century ago. Besides the latest British and American poets and novelists, periodicals, like *Harper's Weekly* that featured drawings of Santa Claus by Thomas Nast and the popular *St. Nicholas* magazine, were readily available from the United States. From England, the *Illustrated London News Christmas Number* was popular, as well as annuals such as *Chum*, *Boys and Girls Own*, and *Leisure Hours*. These sold for about $2.00 each. (Courtesy of PA P 61-225.)

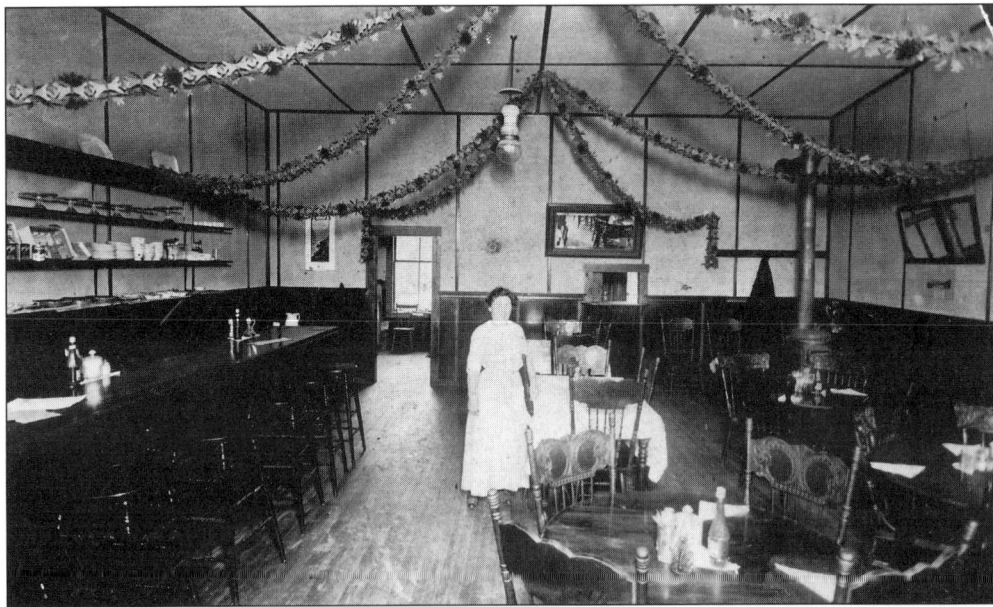

Dining Out Was Popular on Christmas Day! Lindsay's, besides the hotels' dining rooms, was a popular place to eat for Christmas dinner. He loved to advertise using poetry. In 1894 one advertisement read: "Christmas comes but once a year and with it comes good cheer." Following that opening, the poem continued noting that Lindsay's had chicken, goose, turkey, cranberries, mince pies, and plum puddings to offer. He concluded by writing: "Lindsay as a host you'll see, will treat you with civility." (See also page 125.) (Courtesy of PA P 128-190.)

Innovative Merchants in Saint John. Turner and Finlay were leaders in the use of illustrations to promote their stores at 12 King Street and 11 Charlotte, which they ran from 1877 to 1891. Christmas ads were seldom illustrated until the later part of the century. Turner and Finlay used a New York artistic studio, Electrolight Engraving (see also page 14). Most merchants used "word only" advertisements, and their Christmas promotions often ran unchanged until late January. (Courtesy of *Progress*, December 23, 1889.)

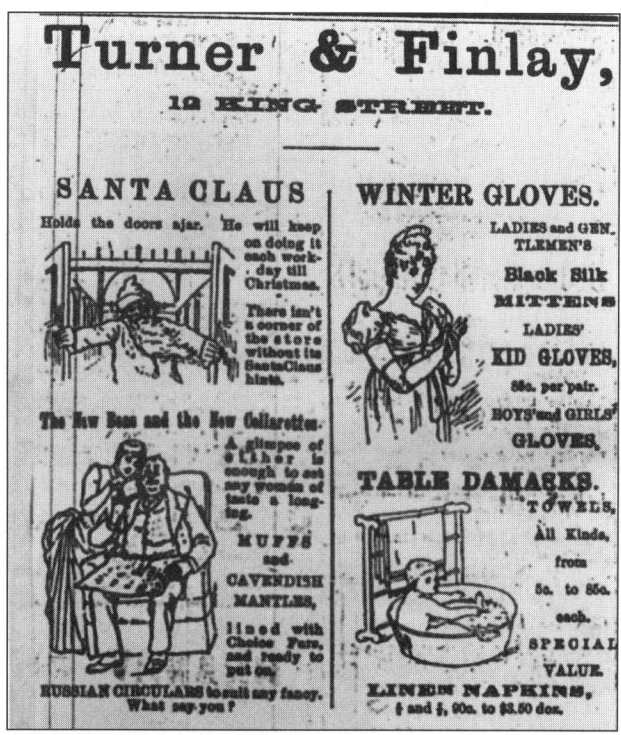

Wilcox Clothing for Men and Women, 1910. Specialty stores with local owners were the rule rather then the exception from the 1860s to the 1950s in New Brunswick. This is the Wilcox store 54–60 Dock Street in 1910. A.V.F. Duffy, the photographer, was courting one of the Wilcox girls; this might explain his interest in the store because the lady in the doorway is possibly the object of his affections. (See photo of G.W. on page 100 and decide for yourself!) (Courtesy of Victor Duffy.)

George Robertson Sends Christmas Greetings. George Robertson was a grocer and the mayor of Saint John in 1894 when this engraving of his 50 King Street store appeared. As mayor, he was busy overseeing the expansion of the Sand Point Docks, featured in the Arcadia book *Saint John West and Its Neighbours*. He also had time to see that his shop was well stocked and lavishly decorated for Christmas. The *Saint John Globe* described his store as having spruce and evergreen banners, and in the windows mistletoe was draped over the Christmas confections and groceries.

Ten
Christmas in the Home

The home was the base from which the observance of Christmas in the community was enjoyed. It is where the pennies were counted before setting out to shop, where lines were learned for school closings or Sunday school parties, where foods were prepared for the feast on the 25th, where cards were written to send to friends, and where friends were entertained around the piano and fed at the festive table. Each household held customs in common with others, such as the decoration of the tree, hanging stockings, and reading favourite poems, prose, or passages of Scripture. As well, there were customs unique to each home, and some of both of these are explored in this chapter. (Courtesy *Halifax Morning Chronicle*, December 27, 1890.)

Cooking to Be Done. The Dufferin House cook in 1924 prepares a pie for the guests of this west Saint John hotel on Rodney Street. It was where many longshoremen working at the port in winter would have their Christmas dinner. (Courtesy of Victor Duffy.)

Letters to Be Written. A.V.F. Duffy identified this photo as "G.W." at her writing desk in 1916. The custom of sending cards, which began with Sir Henry Cole in England in 1846, largely replaced the idea of writing long Christmas letters, which was the norm in the early Victorian era. However, the Victorians still used their writing skills by keeping diaries and journals. (Courtesy of Victor Duffy.)

Carts to Be Hooked Up. Wheeled goods, imitating grown-up versions of transportation devices like trains, carts, and wagons, were popular gifts. This boy's gift has been ingeniously fastened to the family pet by a collar and harness in this 1914 photo from Saint John West. (Courtesy of Victor Duffy.)

Dolls That Needed Fresh Air. Doll carriages were the most popular wheeled gift for girls. In this case, the carriages have been modified to function as sleighs. The girls pictured, Judy and Elizabeth Bastin, are shown in Dalhousie in 1944 setting off for an afternoon of shopping. (Courtesy of Doris Kennedy.)

Prayers to Be Said. The creche was usually seen only in Roman Catholic churches. After World War II, creches began to appear in homes and in some Protestant churches. One of earliest creches was shown in 1957, when Ernie Waring donated a wooden manger and also imported from England the holy family figures for St. George's Church in Saint John West. Folks came from miles to see it! (Courtesy of Vintage Photo and Frame.)

Christmas Weddings to Enjoy. In earliest times, Christmas meetings and New Year weddings were not uncommon. It was the one time of the year when farm and lumber chores were at a standstill and the festive occasions allowed young people to meet. Mistletoe imported from England worked its magic on many who met, and marriages after only a few days of courtship were not uncommon. Joe Michaud was the photographer for this Saint John marriage in the 1940s. (Courtesy of HW: Heritage Saint John.)

Eleven

Outside Seasonal Pursuits

Canadian Winter Girl. In New Brunswick, it is said that the first Christmas was celebrated by Champlain and his band when they spent the winter of 1604–1605 on Dochet's Island on the St. Croix River. It was a dismal Christmas with feuding between Protestants and Catholics. Though Christmas was celebrated with feasting, food later ran out and half of the seventy-nine men perished. Champlain's men were the first settlers of New Brunswick to enjoy outdoor activities to relieve the boredom of Canada's long winter. They skated and snowshoed while on the island, skills introduced by the natives who used these means of travel to gather food. When later settlers arrived in New Brunswick in 1783, they found lots of work to do in the winter. There was ice and firewood to cut and deer to hunt. They also found fun in the snow and added sleighing, sliding, and skiing to Champlain's activities. These activities became especially popular through the 1880s for all ages. The Canadian winter girl shown here is not typical of the style of the day, but a fashionable version used on postcards at the turn of the century. (Courtesy of Central N.B. Woodmen's Museum.)

Think Ahead to Summer. One of the essential tasks of winter before modern refrigeration was the cutting of huge blocks of ice from river and lakeside locations and the storage in sawdust-packed icehouses so that food could be kept from spoiling in the summer months. This photo depicts cutting at Hartland on the St. John River. The third man from the left is V.W. Simms. He needed the ice to manufacture the ice cream that he was well known for in the area. (Courtesy of Doris Kennedy.)

Fox Furs For Sale. Ronald W. Smith is shown in 1925 looking over his father Leonard Smith's fox pelts. Farming foxes was an important form of income in the first few decades of the century, and its revenue made Christmas happier for many a family, like the Smiths. (See young Leonard on page 107.) (Courtesy of Mrs. Claude Babcock.)

Deer Hunters in Albert County. Deer meat and other game were essential sources of food for the family. Mrs. Claude Babcock remembers her mother saying that roast deer meat was a common treat for Christmas dinner. It was also the best meat for mince meat pies and tarts of the season. (Courtesy of Mrs. Claude Babcock.)

A Team at Work. The team of horses could be going into the woods of Albert County to yard logs or could be heading to the lake shown to cut ice or clear it of snow so the family trailing behind could go skating. This picture was taken in 1900. (Courtesy of Mrs. Claude Babcock.)

The Reservoir. Carol Harris of Fairville, now Saint John West, remembers skating on what they called the Reservoir. It was a pond kept by Moosehead Breweries on the lower end of Ready Street. (Courtesy of Carol Harris.)

New Coat from Old. Winter coats were a necessity for children to enjoy the outdoors. Glenna Jack remembers her mom, Lillian Cathlin, taking a donated woman's wool coat and fashioning her daughter an itchy, but warm coat for Christmas in 1939. (Courtesy of Glenna Jack.)

Coasting, a Popular Diversion Everywhere. Coasting at Sussex Corner in 1926 are, from left to right, Franklin Smith, Ralph Styles, and Ronald Smith. A pin sticker sled from Eaton's cost only 15¢ when this picture was taken c. 1910. A top-of-the-line sled like the one in the middle cost $1.25. Sleds and horses seemed to co-exist in the country, but in the city of Saint John, councillors felt car traffic necessitated setting nine of the steepest hills aside for safe sledding from 2 to 5 pm and 7 to 9 pm daily during the winter months. The Boy Scouts patrolled these hills to ensure safety. (Courtesy of Mrs. Claude Babcock.)

Entrancing Icicles. In 1902 in Grangeville in Kent County, Leonard Smith is entranced by the icicles formed on his dad's shed. Leonard Smith became the owner of the fox furs that his son is admiring on page 104. (Courtesy of Mrs. Claude Babcock.)

A New Year's Boat Race at Dalhousie. New Brunswickers are a hardy lot and adaptable at finding winter diversions. In the south of the province, there are records of tugboat excursions well into January up the St. John River when it was ice free. In this New Year's Day, 1913 photo, a boat race at Dalhousie is in progress on the open waters of the Bay of Chaleur. (Courtesy of PA P 28-11.)

Skillen's Postcard of Skating in St. Martins. A pair of skates strapped to a pair of boots could be bought for 50¢, less if they could be found secondhand. These skaters at St. Martins may be on Whelpley skates; Whelpley was a manufacturer at Greenwich on the St. John River who in some years manufactured 16,600 pairs of skates, exporting half to the U.S. His main competitor was the Starr Company of Halifax, who produced skates with nostalgic names like Micmac, Chebucto, Beaver, and Starr at $1 to $5 a pair. (Courtesy of PA P 22-157.)

Racing on the Miramichi. At Newcastle, the famed Miramichi is used in winter for an iceboat race. Those on such craft moved as fast as man could in the days when wooden ships, like the one frozen in the ice in the background, were still the main means of travel. (Courtesy of PA P 18-23.)

Curlers Pose at the Thistle Rink. Curling, a Scottish game, was a popular Christmas Day activity on Lily Lake in Saint John, on the St. John River, and at the Officer's Square in Fredericton. In 1883 John Neill of Gibson, founder of the Fredericton Curling Club in 1854 and then the oldest curler in the province, was honoured by being asked to deliver a shot declaring the season open on New Year's Day. These curlers are in the Thistle Curling Club, Saint John, built in 1880. It was the first indoor curling club in the Maritimes. (Courtesy of PA P 52-3.)

Speedskating: a Very Popular Sport. Rose Johnston (on the left) poses at a speedskating meet in Moncton in February 1923. Such speedskating competitions brought skilled competitors to the Moncton and the East End rink in Saint John (shown below on February 21, 1921) from all across Canada. Besides speedskating, there was barrel jumping and one-legged skating demonstrations. (Courtesy of Moncton photo to PA P 75-24F and Saint John to Victor Duffy.)

Ice Palace For Canadian Queen. This ice palace was constructed at the "Head of King" on the edge of King's Square and was done to mark the winter carnival in Saint John in 1923, the year the first-ever Miss Canada, Winnifred Blair, of Saint John, was crowned. The WCTU water fountain and monument is behind the ice blocks. It was considered the city's ugliest structure and is well hidden behind the greenery.

Skating Carnivals, a Popular Winter Activity. Communities of all sizes held winter skating carnivals as a way to encourage outdoor involvement during the dark, cold winter season. Here four "horsewomen" in Hartland are dressed for the Ice Parade in winter of 1922–23. They are, from left to right, Helen Raymond, Ethel MacIntosh, Elsa Keith, and Jen Boyer. They would have spent days making these costumes for the parade. (Courtesy of Doris Kennedy.)

Hockey: Popular on Outdoor Rinks Only. Hockey took a while to gain popularity, and when the first indoor rink, the Victoria in Saint John, was built in 1883, it was not equipped for the game. Most were content to play on the rivers and lakes. The skaters shown from St. George are, from left to right: (kneeling) M. Stewart, J. Clinch, T. Mooney, and G. Reardon; (standing) H. Allen, E. McGratton, D. Meeting, H. Maxwell, C. Doyle, W. MacDonald, and E. Lynch. Josephine Campbell took the picture in 1931. (Courtesy of Elizabeth Toy.)

Marvelling at the Ice Chunks. The New Brunswick winter provides an ever-changing landscape which invites housebound explorers out for adventure. Harry Sharpe is shown among huge chunks of the frozen St. John River that have built up at what is now the base of the Hartland covered bridge in 1913 before it was boarded and roofed. (Courtesy of Doris Kennedy.)

Twelve

Lending a Helping Hand

The Christmas Kettle. The churches, hospitals, and social clubs, those with local roots or national and international connections, did their best to see that those who were sick, alone, or institutionalised were able to share the joys of the Christmas season. It was in the Victorian era that several organisations, still functioning today, were founded, including the Salvation Army as represented by the lady (to the right) jingling her bells in hopes of good donations from Saint Johners. In this chapter we learn of agencies whose aim may be summed up by this sentiment from the *Saint John Globe* of December 27, 1884: "The Christmas holidays impose much worth and worry upon all sorts and conditions of men. It gives the opportunity for display of much kind and beautiful feelings, but it calls forth much extra work, of extra care for others welfare, of extra thought for others happiness, all, no doubt, gladly performed." (Courtesy of Salvation Army: George Scott Railton Heritage Centre Archives.)

Lavish Interior Decorations. Saint John established the first Lunatic Asylum in Canada in 1835 on a highland overlooking the mouth of the Saint John River, then a tranquil setting considered helpful to the restoration of health to the patients. In 1997 the building was still in use as a centre for the mentally ill. In these turn-of-the-century photos, the Asylum, then its proper name, was decorated for the season by staff and patients well enough to offer their assistance. (Courtesy of New Brunswick Nurses Association.)

Staff Party in the Old Gym. The patients not confined to their rooms could enjoy many musical and dramatic presentations by community groups in the auditorium. Musicians, entertainers, and the several hundred who worked in the asylum knew of the decorations and compassionate care the patients received. (Courtesy of New Brunswick Nurses Association.)

Borrowing an Idea From the Church. Other than the area churches, few places would have been decorated as well as the Provincial Asylum at Simms Corner in Saint John. The spruce tips would have been gathered at the Annex farm on Sand Cove Road, where dairy cows were kept and crops raised by the patients able to work. The twisted crepe paper was a favourite Victorian-era decoration. The cardstock "GREETINGS" on the greens was an idea churches used extensively in their sanctuaries. (Courtesy of New Brunswick Nurses Association.)

Students at Barnhill Involved in Port Project. Lew Harrison took this photo on December 16, 1952, of students involved in a Canadian Red Cross program at Barnhill School in the Parish of Lancaster, now Saint John West. They were preparing gifts for immigrants arriving by boat to the port. (Courtesy of Canadian Red Cross.)

Saint John High Students Greet Immigrants. A group of students, photographed by Lew Harrison, from Saint John High School are shown decorating a tree at the Red Cross room of the Immigration building in Saint John West in preparation for immigrants from Europe who would arrive by boat in the mid-1950s; this was before ice breaking kept the port of Montreal open all winter, or jet aircraft took most of them to central Canada. (Courtesy of Canadian Red Cross.)

Two Ways of Helping Out. In these mid-1950s photos, Santa and Red Cross students greet the kids who have arrived in the port of Saint John. These children would have been more familiar with the robed and mitre-carrying St. Nicholas of Europe than with the North American version of a furry Santa based on Thomas Nast's late nineteenth-century drawings. (Courtesy of Canadian Red Cross.)

Two Facets of Christmas Caring in Saint John. On the top left are care packages prepared by students for the Red Cross and sent overseas during World War II. On the bottom, veterans of World War I enjoy Christmas at the Veterans Hospital in Saint John West. (Both photos courtesy of Canadian Red Cross.)

Caroling Is a Time-Honoured Christmas Joy. In the days before radio and television, patients in hospital would seldom hear carols, so nurses would minister to them by holding candlelight carol vigils in the wards, such as this at the Victoria Public Hospital in Fredericton in 1955. In the front row are Jessica Tweedale Hall, instructor; Mary McGinnis, RN, with accordion; and Mr. Manuel, orderly. The singers were probationary and first-year nurses. (Courtesy of New Brunswick Nurses Association.)

Two Hundred and Fifty Kids Await Santa's Attention. A private Protestant orphanage was created by an act of incorporation on April 12, 1855, in Saint John. Each December, caring citizens gave time, money, and gifts to help orphaned children celebrate Christmas. Here, Santa visits the two hundred and fifty kids residing at the New Brunswick Protestants Orphanage Home in the 1950s. (Courtesy of NBPOH.)

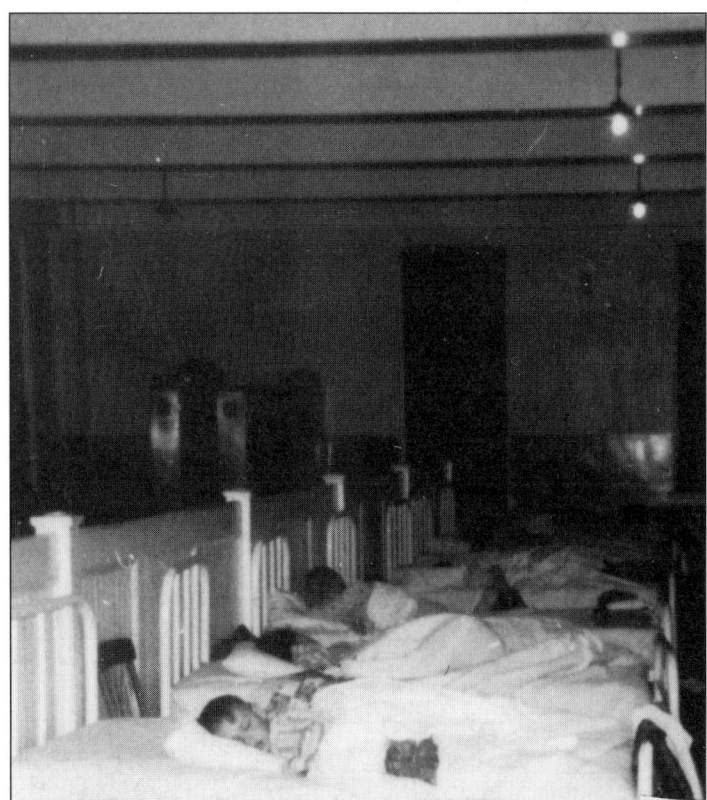

The Children Are Nestled. E.M. Daye eloquently portrays these children at bedtime in his 1931 poem, "The New Brunswick Protestants Orphans' Home," when he writes: "Nestled all safely in warm cozy bed / Each darling baby lays down its sweet head." (Courtesy of NBPOH.)

Christmas Morning at the New Brunswick Protestants Orphanage, 1953. With toys and gifts lined up, Miss Vera Coles and Beatrice McKiel look over the decorated auditorium of the home and await the children's arrival. Miss Coles served for forty-two years at the institution, and on retirement in 1967, it was calculated by Clarence C. Colwell, president at the time, that she had been a mother to four thousand children. (Courtesy of NBPOH.)

Every Boy Wanted to Be a Cowboy. Gene Autrey once visited the New Brunswick Protestants Orphanage, but that was long before these boys received these cowboy outfits This was the dream gift of every boy in the mid-1950s. (Courtesy of NBPOH.)

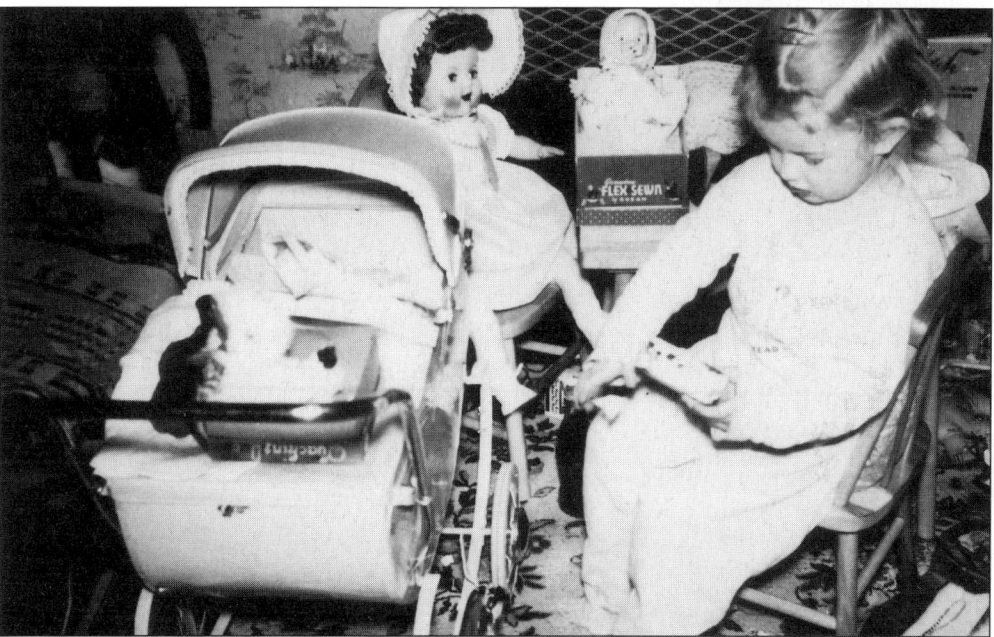

Hearts Opened in December. Reports of the Protestant Orphanage clearly show that December was the month the most donations of gifts and money were received. As part of December routine, service clubs, like the Lancaster Kiwanis, would hold parties for the children, and they would be taken as guests to the Ford Plant party, among others, and also would take the children to movies at the Gaiety Theatre just down the street. Santa would visit, of course, and the gifts he brought this girl would be similar to those received by children in the affluent Quinton Heights and Greendale area that were adjacent to the orphanage property. (See also page 32.) (Courtesy of NBPOH.)

Port Nurse, Christmas, 1921. In the Victorian era, Saint John citizens left their homes on Christmas Day to visit the alms houses, home for the incurables, and the orphanages to bring food and greetings to those that might be forgotten. Though many government social programs exist today, the Victorian concern for the indigent continue to be part of Christmas and programs at churches, through food banks and via appeals like the Empty Stocking Fund and Big Daddies. These are well supported by New Brunswickers. The port nurse no longer greets children, as shown above, but caring continues in many other ways. (Courtesy of Nurses Association of New Brunswick.)

Thirteen
Other December Diversions

This and That. This chapter concludes our look at Christmas in New Brunswick with a collection of this and that—items that just didn't fit neatly into the previous chapters, but which nonetheless still illustrate some facet of Christmas past that is worth noting. We begin with two postcards that Bob Donovan picked up at a flea market. Postcards became a popular way of exchanging Christmas greetings at the beginning of the twentieth century, when it became possible to print full colour cards cheaply due to advancing technological improvements in the printing industry. Also, a card could be sent for 1¢ anywhere in Canada. For the collector, those postcards which circulated locally are of most interest; this is easily determined from the address. Collectors have been known to find cards from past family members or friends when rooting through flea market or yard sale material. These have a greater sentimental and sometimes higher financial value. Finding a card with an obvious error also makes a card more valuable. Can you spot the difference in the cards to the right? (Courtesy of Bob Donovan.)

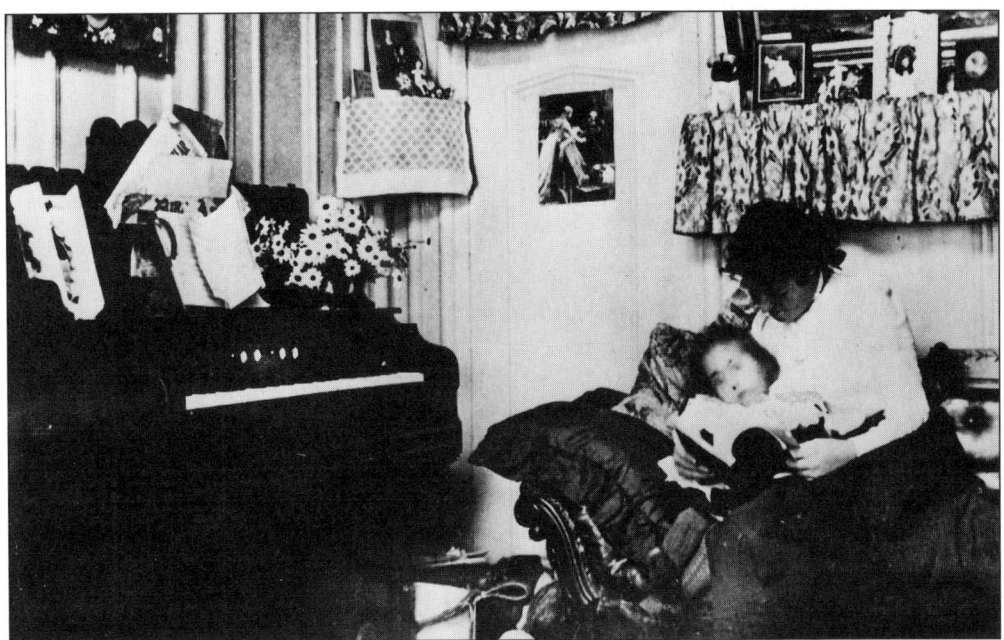

Christmas at Sea. New Brunswickers in the Victorian era had a strong connection with the sea because of the crewmen and officers of the ships built in the province. Captains sometimes took their family to sea for Christmas, as above. If a captain was putting out to sea, he would take provisions with him for the Christmas Day dinner. There would be a tree for the galley and sometimes one for the mast and the bowsprit. (Courtesy of The Yarmouth County Historical Society Museum and Research Library PH 131-A.)

A Christmas Superstition Explained. Scott Sipprelle made the sled in this photo for his children to enjoy for Christmas, 1904. His wife, with their baby Ezekiel, is in the doorway of their home at Victoria Corner. James, Elsa, and Ruth (from left to right) are playing in the yard. Note the greens banked around the house. This was a late fall task designed to keep out drafts. Many believed that the indoor decorative greens had to be removed by Little Christmas and burnt or fed to cattle; otherwise, bad luck would befall the family. (Courtesy of Doris Kennedy.)

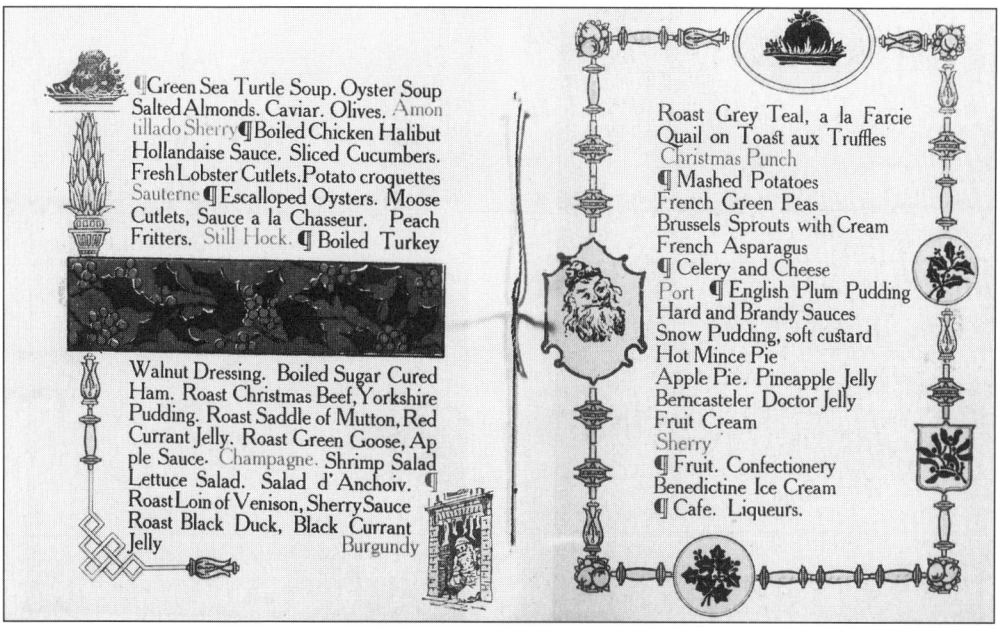

¶Green Sea Turtle Soup. Oyster Soup
Salted Almonds. Caviar. Olives. Amon
tillado Sherry ¶Boiled Chicken Halibut
Hollandaise Sauce. Sliced Cucumbers.
Fresh Lobster Cutlets. Potato croquettes
Sauterne ¶Escalloped Oysters. Moose
Cutlets, Sauce a la Chasseur. Peach
Fritters. Still Hock. ¶Boiled Turkey

Walnut Dressing. Boiled Sugar Cured
Ham. Roast Christmas Beef, Yorkshire
Pudding. Roast Saddle of Mutton, Red
Currant Jelly. Roast Green Goose, Ap
ple Sauce. Champagne. Shrimp Salad
Lettuce Salad. Salad d' Anchoiv. ¶
Roast Loin of Venison, Sherry Sauce
Roast Black Duck, Black Currant
Jelly   Burgundy

Roast Grey Teal, a la Farcie
Quail on Toast aux Truffles
Christmas Punch
¶ Mashed Potatoes
French Green Peas
Brussels Sprouts with Cream
French Asparagus
¶ Celery and Cheese
Port ¶ English Plum Pudding
Hard and Brandy Sauces
Snow Pudding, soft custard
Hot Mince Pie
Apple Pie. Pineapple Jelly
Berncasteler Doctor Jelly
Fruit Cream
Sherry
¶ Fruit. Confectionery
Benedictine Ice Cream
¶ Cafe. Liqueurs.

The Menu of the Royal Hotel in Saint John, 1901. Hotel menus were usually printed in the newspaper columns of the daily papers of the three major cities of the province. Along with the bill of fare served, the editorial copy would indicate how extensive the decorations were at the various establishments. The year this menu appeared, the *Daily Sun* noted: "There are men in many parts of Canada and the United States who look forward for twelve months to the joy of eating their Christmas dinner in St. John. The Royal has a name from ocean to ocean, and so have all the other hostelries of the city."

Christmas Cards. This group of cards is representative of those available at the turn of the century, and they illustrate both sacred and secular themes. On December 9, 1884, the *Saint John Globe* advised mail for England had to be posted that day. The paper suggested "sets" of cards to illustrate Canadian life to the overseas recipients, such as ones titled "Snow shoes," "Toboggan," "Snowball," and "Carnival" for only 2¢ a set. Can you spot a problem with this collection?

Christmas Cakes.

1 lb. butter
2 lbs. sugar
6 eggs
1 teaspoon soda
2 " " cream of tartar.
1/2 teacup water
1 grated nutmeg.
flour to make pretty stiff.
(mixture to be kneaded by
hand.)

Caraway seed may be
added as desired.

From mss. 'cook-book' of
Mrs. A. McN. Travis, 1867.

A Flea Market Find. To the left is a recipe for a Christmas cake enjoyed in 1867 by Mrs. A. McN Travis. Below is a card that A.D. Ganong selected from a group of seven artist by A.Y. Jackson which turned up at a flea market and made an interesting find. The Ganong Company of St. Stephen has been making Christmas chocolates for more than a century.

· To · Greet · You ·

A WISH SINCERE FOR
A HAPPY CHRISTMAS AND
A NEW YEAR FULL
OF CHEER

GANONG BROS., LTD.

A. D. Ganong
President.

Christmas Parties. The custom of employers giving lavish Christmas parties began in the Victorian era, and it was also customary for the employees to give the owner and/or boss a suitable token of appreciation. One of Saint John's oldest firms, T.S. Simms and Co., was still following this tradition when this photo was taken at Tom Simms home at 325 Lancaster Avenue about 1940. (Courtesy of HW: Simms collection #884.)

Newspaper Gathering. More informally, the staff of the *Evening Times Globe* in Saint John has just put the December 24th issue on the streets and has gathered with Santa in the newsroom on Canterbury Street to enjoy some libations in celebration of the season. Around the table, we see staff members of the 1950s, including Don Smith, Helmer Biermann ,Doug Costello, Santa, Foster Marr, and Gussie Fewing. (Courtesy of HW: Richards collection PIRP 5684.)

A Last Look at the Festive Season. On the left is Charlotte Street with festive lights. On the right is the Irving tree in the Loyalist Burial Grounds, a new custom that has built on a 1920s tradition of lighting a huge tree in the King's Square. Below, and our final picture, is a "Merry Christmas" greeting that no longer hangs in Saint John, but is our wish to you as we conclude this look at Christmas in New Brunswick.